SHANKLY

SHANKLY
Bill Shankly

ARTHUR BARKER LIMITED   LONDON
A subsidiary of Weidenfeld (Publishers) Limited

Published in Great Britain by Arthur Barker Limited
11 St John's Hill, London SW11

ISBN 0 213 16603 8

Printed in Great Britain by
Willmer Brothers Limited, Birkenhead

Contents

List of Illustrations

In memory of my parents and in tribute to my wife and family and all the people I worked for and worked with, especially the people of the city of Liverpool.

Foreword

It is my privilege to lead you into the life story of Bill Shankly, the Scottish character who made mountains out of molehills and men.

'Discipline', 'dedication', 'enthusiasm' and 'success' are words synonymous with this soccer fanatic who turned his dreams into an amazing career without once losing touch with the people who pay at the turnstiles.

Bill is a man one comes to know gradually and tentatively, by learning how to humour a Vesuvian temperament. I can best illustrate this point with a couple of anecdotes.

The first is from a period when he was fascinated by Robert Stack's television characterization of the 1920s American gangbuster, Eliot Ness.

I was sent to Liverpool by my sports editor on the *Daily Express* the morning after a defeat by Leicester City in the FA Cup. The task was to measure reaction to an incident in which goal-scoring star Roger Hunt had thrown his red jersey into the trainers' dugout after being singled out to become the club's first ever substituted player.

It was a cold, grey day, and I wore a hound's-tooth overcoat with a fur collar. As I reached the narrow corridor which led to the inquiries window at the old Liverpool ground, the club secretary, Peter Robinson, moved across from his office.

'I hope you are not on the mission I think you're on,' he said.

I told him I was, and he smiled and said, 'Well, I won't throw you out myself, I'll leave it to Bill.'

Bill made several fleeting appearances, nipping across the corridor from office to office until he paused and asked, 'Are you looking for somebody?' I said I was looking for him.

'What can I do for you?'

'About last night . . .'

'Last night? What about last night?'

'Roger Hunt . . .'

This caused an eruption, beginning with the accusation, 'You're not here to talk about one of my players, are you?' and developing into an animated farce of finger-wagging and marching and retreating.

Bill did the finger-wagging and marching – out of the corridor and into the foyer, into the kitchen and back into the foyer – while I retreated, eventually backing out of the main door saying apologetically, 'All right, Bill, all right . . .'

Later, other journalists went to visit him in strength, and he told them: 'I had your man Roberts round this morning and I sent him away with a flea in his ear – in his Untouchables overcoat!'

Some years later, Tommy Smith walked out on the Liverpool team at Highbury after being dropped for a match against Arsenal. Once again I was the intrepid investigator, though better armed this time.

The new stadium had been completed, and I found Bill taking a shower in the trainers' quarters.

'What brings you here?' he asked, pointedly.

'Just passing through,' I lied.

As he towelled himself down we talked about Sir Matt Busby's autobiography, *Soccer at the Top*, which was about to be published. We then moved next door into Bill's office, talked about Sir Matt some more and then moved on to discuss Stan Cullis, Tom Finney, and other sundry personalities.

'We'll have a cup of tea,' Bill decided at last, and we moved back into the trainers' quarters, where he filled an electric kettle, plugged it in and added a few more words about Stan Cullis.

When the tea was made, he poured and asked: 'Sugar?'
'No, thank you,' I said.
'Milk?'
'Please.'

As my tea turned from black to brown he said, 'I suppose you want to know about Tommy Smith?'

Having experienced Bill and his moods in triumph and disappointment, I was fascinated by the place of his origin, so I went to Scotland to see for myself.

Old John Shankly told his family of a bygone minister called Peden who prophesied that the end of the world would be nigh when the church of Glenbuck had no roof and sheep roamed around its pews.

In 1976 the grey stone church was derelict and overgrown with moss. It had a congregation of animal food-stuff (the store of a local farmer), had been a sanctuary for chickens, and sheep were grazing close to its door. The roof was still intact only because David Crawford, a villager but not locally born, had once been refused permission to dismantle it and put the timbers to other uses.

David was in ill health and missed the companionship of his friends, who had moved to Muirkirk, three miles along the road to Ayr. In February 1976 he decided to join them. He left the cottage, 'Rowanbank', taking with him his wife, Elizabeth.

Elizabeth, daughter of John Shankly and sister of the man whose story you are about to read, was the last of the children of Glenbuck. No more than twenty people, all immigrant, occupied its twelve remaining houses, eight of which were set in two slate-grey, rough-cut pre-1938 council blocks. Elizabeth, who had paid fifty pounds for Rowanbank in 1939, was seventy years old.

'Need I try to tell you how my husband and I feel after my lifetime in Glenbuck and our thirty-seven years of married life in the same house?' she said. 'We have shed a few tears these last few days, but the happy memories for us will never die.'

In the 1870s the industrial revolution brought a community to the undulating Scottish countryside. Before this there had been lead mines, but the need for coal gave Glenbuck life, and it once had a population of 1200.

Glenbuck grew and receded with the mining industry until it became a spectre in the hills, an almost pointless detour from the A 70 road, by courtesy of John Macadam.

The road up to the village followed the skirting of gentle Glenbuck Loch, three-quarters of a mile long, and a warning to motorists on the A 70 to 'heed your speed'. The narrow road, flanked by scarred hillsides, wound down and around past the Crawford cottage and the ruins came into view on the right-hand side; stark headstones in a valley of forgotten graves.

First there was the old school, and water gushing from a near-by spring. An old bicycle stood at the side of a wall and the inevitable sheep were in strength on land at the back.

The front of the building was a series of casualties; the first window space was boarded up, the second, larger, had glass covering all but a section at the top, the third was smashed in two places and the fourth was a gaping space, with not even the remnants of a frame.

Inside, where children once struggled with maths and language, and were regaled with stories of Scottish heroes, the seat of learning had also given way to the dietary needs of livestock.

Next there was the gaunt, deserted minister's house and the church, awesome in neglect but given some relief by trees standing by like loyal sentinels. Padlocked iron gates at the front of the church were mocked by the rubble of a wrecked wall and a breach leading only to a slope thick with undergrowth. Here, a small rock monument was engraved: 'Erected by the people of Glenbuck to commemorate the sixtieth year of Her Majesty's reign, 22 June 1897.'

In contrast a prominent plaque under the church windows proclaimed: 'This stone is placed here by Charles Howatson, of Glenbuck, to commemorate the noble life and heroic death of John Brown, Richard Cameron and others, who were killed (1680–85) in these martyr districts for faithfulness to the cause of Christ in Church and State. This church was opened for public worship 16 July 1882.'

A memorial, like many dotted about the hills, recalled 'The Killing Times', when Covenanters like Brown and Cameron were slain by Dragoons.

Alongside the church was what used to be the schoolmaster's house, now occupied by the owner of a private mine. Then there was a clearing, taken over by clinging rough grass, where once stood Auchenstilloch Cottages—'The Monkey Row'—the second of which provided shelter for John and Barbara Shankly and their family of ten. Foundations of homes, gutted and smashed into fragments of brick and mortar recycled in the building of roads, were still evident below the pygmean jungle.

The space ended abruptly, alongside another deceased building, the old village hall, once the heart of community spirit, debate and entertainment, now just another farming outhouse, a landmark for the sheep, grazing on below great Hareshaw Hill.

Across the road from this desolate scene there was a bus stop, a stone wall, a burn, telegraph poles, rusted relics of children's swings and hills in waves out to the horizon. Here was Glenbuck's greatest deception to the eyes of strangers, for the marshy land, almost knee-deep in rushes, sloping down from the wall, was the ground of Glenbuck's famous football players, the Cherrypickers: Burnside Park.

Cherrypickers? The club was founded in the late 1870s by Edward Bone, William Brown, 'and others'. It was originally called 'Glenbuck Athletic', with colours of white jerseys and black shorts. Its first ground was lost when one of the pit shafts was sunk. Its second was on the hillside. Then it was decided that Burnside was the most level patch in the village.

The title changed at the turn of the century, when 'Cherrypickers', at first a nickname, was adopted officially. The origins of this are still somewhat cloudy, though there is no doubt that it alluded to the 11th Hussars and their cherry-coloured breeches. During the Peninsular War in Spain, the Hussars arrived one day at a Spanish village. They were hot and weary and stripped in a nearby cherry orchard.

In Glenbuck one story goes that Tom Menzies and his brother strutted about the street as youngsters, wearing their caps after the manner of Hussars and proclaiming they were 'Cherry-pickers'. Another tale tells how the boys of the village would gather around Milliken's store in the evenings and talk of football. One summer evening there was a large basket of cherries in the yard, but when the boys went home the basket was empty. Whatever else, it is almost certain that men from Glenbuck or Muirkirk served with the Hussars in the Boer War in 1900.

The club was run by an elected committee and John Shankly was closely connected with its affairs as it grew into a legend in Scottish junior football. It was a family club, where names like Tait, Bone, Knox, Menzies and Wallace recurred and most players had nicknames. There was once a half-back line of Bush Menzies, Push Menzies and Biscuit Blyth.

Fifty players from Glenbuck progressed to senior football, including the five brothers Shankly – Alec (Ayr United, Clyde); James (Portsmouth, Carlisle, Sheffield United, Southend United, Barrow); John (Portsmouth, Blackpool, Alloa); Bob (Alloa, Tunbridge Wells, Falkirk); and Bill (Carlisle, Preston).

Bill, who had a trial for the Cherrypickers shortly before the club folded, was one of six players from the village who went on to represent Scotland. The others were his brother Bob, William Muir, Alec Brown, George Halley and John Crosbie. Bill was most honoured, making thirteen appearances between 1938 and 1943 (five full and eight wartime internationals)

Alec Tait played for the Tottenham team that won the original gold FA Cup in 1901. Later that year the trophy was brought to Glenbuck and displayed in a shop-window. Four years later it was stolen from a Birmingham shop-window, while in possession of Aston Villa, and was never recovered.

Alec Brown played for Scotland against England on the day of the 1902 Ibrox disaster. Bobby Templeton of Kilmarnock made a run down the right wing, worked the ball into the middle and passed to Brown, who scored. The tragedy occurred at that moment, when part of the stand collapsed and twenty-five people were killed.

The wall opposite the church was a good vantage-point for watching the Cherrypickers and occasional suggestions that the referee be thrown into the burn were sometimes acted upon. Now there was just a George VI post-box attached to a telegraph-pole (collections 10.15 am, Monday to Saturday; no collection Sunday or New Year's Day). Further along the left-hand side of the road was a telephone box, facing the tracks leading up to what was left of the local mining industry.

Viaduct Mine still gave up some 150 tons of coal a day, while over the brae production was less ambitious, a thirteen-man operation, with four at the coal face combining to yield forty tons a day.

The sign 'Grasshill Mine' was askew on a rusty pole, leaning towards the ground, and the message was repeated in white paint on a coal-black piece of felting beside a boulder and a discarded empty bottle, 'Bell's Old Scotch Whisky, extra special'.

A weighing platform stood beside an old blue hut, and the path of slag climbed up to where Bill Shankly began his working life. The pit was filled in, but higher still, past rusted old machinery and a heap of rubber tyres, was the mine, where sixty-three-year-old Jim Short still laboured in steel helmet with lamp, working on the engine that pulled up the wagons of coal.

Jim had moved from Glenbuck to Muirkirk in 1951. 'I had to leave, because they pulled the house down,' he said. He had grown up alongside the Shanklys, had been at school with Bill and had worked with him at the pit. 'He was just the same then as he is now,' said Jim. 'Hardy and go-ahead. If he had an objective, he always got to it.'

From Grasshill, Glenbuck looked even more of a corpse, but Jim still loved to be around the place. 'I was once redundant for three years and I spent most of my days here, walking seven miles up the back road from Muirkirk and walking seven miles back again. Nostalgia, you see.'

We stood beside Stottencleugh Burn, a tributary of the river Ayr. 'Burns wrote of the river in spate or flood, "From Glenbuck down to the Rattonkeys, auld Ayr was just but one tumbling sea," ' Jim recalled.

The sight of the village in 1976 would no doubt have saddened the poet's eyes and prompted a pitying verse. But it was not always like this; once families abounded in the valley and brought life to Rabbie's words :

> Gie me ae spark o' Nature's fire,
> That's a' the learning I desire.

JOHN ROBERTS
May 1976

1 Life in Glenbuck

I was born in a little coal-mining village called Glenbuck, about a mile from the Ayrshire-Lanarkshire border, where the Ayrshire road was white and the Lanarkshire road was red shingle. We were not far from the racecourses at Ayr, Lanark, Hamilton Park and Bogside.

Ours was like many other mining villages in Scotland in 1913. By the time I was born the population had decreased to seven hundred, perhaps less. People would move to other villages, four or five miles away, where the mines were possibly better.

I had four brothers, Alec, or 'Sandy' as we called him, Jimmy, John and Bob, and five sisters, Netta, Elizabeth, Isobel, Barbara and Jean. I was the youngest boy and the second youngest in the family. All the boys became professional footballers and once, when we were all at our peaks, we could have beaten any five brothers in the world.

At first the family lived in a two-apartment house. Then, as we grew, we got the house next door and knocked a hole through the adjoining wall to make four apartments. Sometimes we slept six in a room, with hole-in-the-wall beds and, below them, camp-beds that pulled out.

Everyone in the village knew everyone else and the doors were ever open. My mother's key was in the outside of the front door morning, noon and night, so you could have walked into our house any time you wanted to. You could walk into anyone's house and say, 'Good evening, Mrs Smith,' or 'Mrs Davidson' or 'Mrs Brown.'

My mother's name was Barbara – Barbara Gray Blyth before she married. Her brother Robert played for Rangers and Portsmouth, where he became chairman, and her other brother, William, played for Preston and Carlisle, where he became a director. My mother was my greatest inspiration.

First and foremost, she brought up ten children and they were all born at home, which I think is a miracle. To bring up such a large family in our circumstances must have been a terribly hard job for her. She never had very much, but what she had she was willing to share with anybody else. She had no enemies. I have never heard anybody say anything against her.

She was always calm, never lost her temper and was so loyal to her family. Latterly, only my brother John and my mother were left at home. John was working at a pit some distance away, and he did not get home until eleven o'clock at night. He was always working on the afternoon shift and I remember how my mother used to watch for the lights of the bus coming over the hill, bringing John home. Then she would get his supper ready.

In the end she lived for my brother John, who had an unfortunate life, including a lot of heart trouble, and who was the only one of us who did not get married.

John was the middle brother and the smallest, at five feet six inches. He went to Portsmouth as a teenager and I think the training must have been a bit too much for him. He went to Luton from there and was leading goal-scorer. Then he suffered from an overstrained heart muscle. He played for a long time afterwards, but was never the same. He went back home and played for Alloa and then went back to the pit.

My mother was a month off being eighty when she died, not long after she had fallen downstairs. I was manager of Huddersfield Town when she passed away. I received the news by telephone, and I cried. Suddenly I felt a long way from home.

John died just after the Real Madrid–Eintracht European Cup Final at Hampden Park in 1960. He had a heart attack in the stand and was taken from the ground to the Victoria Hospital, Glasgow, during the match, and died that night.

Though my mother was proud of her family, she did not boast and always had time for others. She used to visit relatives in a place called Douglas, where my father was born, seven miles away in Lanarkshire. Maybe five or six of us would go with her and walk to Douglas and back. She would think nothing of that. And she would give away her last penny or her last stitch of clothing.

She used to go to Glasgow on the train to see her sister and her sister would come from Glasgow to our village and perhaps see a coat or something belonging to one of the kids. It was maybe too small for them or too big for them and she would say, 'Look at this, Barbara,' and my mother would say to my aunt, 'Take it, you can have it.' She would give anything away.

I don't think people returned the compliment because I remember I once fancied a bike belonging to my cousin at Yoker. It was a lady's bike. I learnt to ride it and was desperate to get it so my mother paid a pound for it and three shillings and sixpence to bring it home on the train. She couldn't afford it, but she paid for the bike because I wanted it. And they'd had lots of stuff from her.

My father, John, was a postman for a part of his life, but for as long as I can remember him he was a high-class tailor of handmade suits. Tailoring was in his blood. All my relatives and all my sisters could make dresses and alter skirts. I can remember them sewing and darning everything. My father also used to do small jobs in the village, altering clothes for people. If you could alter clothes you could make a bigger living out of that than out of making clothes.

Sometimes when he had done a job for someone in the village the person would ask, 'How much is it?'

'Two shillings,' my father would say.

'Oh, I've only got a shilling, Johnny,' they would say.

'Oh, it's all right,' he would say. 'Pay it some other time.' And he would never bother about it.

I don't know what his wages would have been, but he did not keep much for himself. He didn't smoke or drink. The only thing he did for relaxation was go to the pictures. He loved the pictures. He used to walk four miles there and four miles back. There were never more than two or three wage-packets coming into the house at the same time and my father used to work on clothes for the family, changing long pants into short pants and making dresses for the girls.

He was a fighting man. Not in the sense that he would go looking for trouble. No. But he was spirited. If you had said anything critical about Scotland or his family he would probably have killed you! You would sometimes get the impression that he was a militant man. But he was dead honest, a straightforward man who had no time for fools or practical jokers.

My father did not play football, except at a juvenile level, but he was an athlete, a quarter-miler. He only ran locally, but he was hard to catch – even in his older days. He never lost the skill.

There were four years between all the boys, and the order of the family was boy-girl, boy-girl, and so on.

Alec, my eldest brother, was twenty years older than me. He played for Ayr United before the First World War. Then he was in the Royal Scottish Fusiliers. After the war he was troubled by sciatica and went back to the pits. Eventually he finished and was not working at all. Alec was a lean man, about five feet nine inches tall.

Jimmy, who was four years younger than Alec, could have been one of the finest centre forwards ever born. Sheffield United bought him from Carlisle United for £1,000, which was a big fee then.

He was five feet eleven, thirteen and a half stone and as strong as a bull, but was possibly a victim of circumstances. Jimmy was good in the air and could belt the ball with both feet, but there were a lot of great players then. The teams were full of them. Sheffield United had players like Jimmy Dunne, Freddie Tunstall and Billy Gillespie. So Jimmy went to Southend United for six seasons and was leading goal-scorer for six seasons. He played his best football in the Third Division (South).

He was a big help to the family. Southend paid him eight pounds in the winter and six pounds in the summer. He would come home for the summer and his money helped to keep us all. He helped us during the winter too.

Jimmy's last season was at Barrow, where he played with a bad heel. His League goal-scoring record of thirty-nine in a season still holds at Barrow. Jimmy's last season was my first season at Preston, in 1933.

He went back home with his wife from Yorkshire, who is now a schoolteacher, and we helped him to buy a wagon and start a coal business because he had helped us so much.

Bob, four years younger than John, whom I have already written about, played for Falkirk for seventeen years and then became manager of Falkirk and manager of Dundee. Our careers ran parallel. I played for Preston when Bob played for Falkirk. He took Dundee into the European Cup in 1962 and they scored eight goals against Cologne. Dundee had a tremendous team, with players like Ian Ure, Alan Gilzean and Jimmy Gabriel. Bob later became manager of Hibernian and is now general manager and director of Stirling Albion.

Bob is about five feet ten inches and looks the most like me. He is a quiet type, but that does not mean he is not interested. Bob is a genuine fellow, a one-hundred-per-cent man.

If the whole world was like my family, there would be no trouble, and I am not just being kind to my folks when I make that statement.

Times were hard when I was a boy and we were hungry, especially in the wintertime. There were farms all around us and we used to steal the potatoes and turnips and cabbages and everything. The village policeman had an awful job. We used to know his every movement. We had spies. The farmers were watching for us, but there was a lot of territory to cover and, when it was getting dark at night, it was hard for them to see!

A chap used to come with his big wagon from Strathaven, a beautiful village near Hamilton. He sold loaves, scones, cakes, currant-cakes – they were brilliant, the currant-cakes – biscuits, milk, all sorts of things. And we used to take things from his wagon.

One night we took a whole bunch of bananas from the wagon

of a fruiterer from Clydeside – the biggest bunch you could ever imagine. It took four or five of us to carry it and the bananas lasted for weeks.

Other times we would go to the pits and help ourselves to a bag of coal from the hundreds of tons that were there.

We knew we were doing wrong, but we did not think of it as stealing really. It was devilment more than badness. When we had nothing and took something we did not call it stealing. We were hungry. We needed to satisfy our appetites.

Our parents were too proud even to think we were poor and they would never imagine their children had been pilfering. 'Oh, no, not our Jimmy!' If we had owed a millionaire a penny we would have been told, 'Pay him!' But there is a moral in all this, because when we grew up we realized that some of the things we had done as boys were wrong, but we had learned from the mistakes and possibly that made us better people in the long run. If you go through life doing more good than bad that should tip the scales in your favour.

My father was a man of character and he disciplined us. We were frightened of him of course. Some boys today are not frightened of their fathers and that's a bad job.

Once, when I had misbehaved at school, one of the teachers, Mr Kirkwood, said, 'Do you want your punishment from me or your father?'

'From you,' I told him.

That is the kind of respect I had for my father. Everyone should respect their father. Later in life you can use the lessons you learned as a youngster to help you deal with the young. I had a code to live up to as an athlete. I had to be fit and behave myself. And when I became a manager I had a code of discipline for footballers. But I didn't put anybody in jail or fine them. I had my way of doing things and it was mainly based on mutual respect.

At the village school the form mistress would give you the leather strap over your hand if you did something wrong. If you put out your hand and laughed at her, that made it worse. But if you did anything above that you were taken through to the Big

Man, the headmaster, who was called Mr John Roger.

He was about six feet and he would look at you and rub his hands. He had a stock phrase, 'Woe betide you.' He said it quietly, menacingly. Boy, did he frighten the life out of you! He lashed you six times on your hands, and if you were sarcastic with him he would give you six more.

One day Mr Roger went out of the classroom for a while. There was a big clock high on the wall and I thought it would be a good idea to put the time forward by half an hour so that we could get out of school early. It was eleven o'clock and we were due to be out at twelve. I had to climb to the top of ladders to get to the clock, and I changed the time to eleven-thirty. But before I could climb down again, Mr Roger walked back into the room.

'Oh, you're there, Shankly,' he said in the voice that made us quake. Naturally I feared the worst. But instead of bringing me down for a lashing, he made me sit at the top of the ladders for an hour, and it was a difficult job for me to balance up there.

The other boys were nearly killing themselves with laughter – and Mr Roger clipped one or two round the ears. He made an example of me in front of the class, and he knew that would probably hurt me more than hitting me. We always put a cocky look on our faces, like little gangsters, when he told us to put our hands out. We wouldn't show pain, even though it was killing us.

By leaving me up on top of the ladders he was making a show of me. You see, Mr Roger knew us and he knew he was helping us. What he did was character-building. He knew that deep down what we did was in mischief. Everyone was frightened of him, but if you are not afraid there is something wrong with you. You are very tough, very ignorant, very vain or very spoiled.

I went to school from the age of five till I was fourteen, which was the usual thing in those days. My favourite subject was geography. I wanted to know all about England and all about Europe. I have always had a good memory and at school I was pretty sharp. Anything I was interested in I kept in my head. If I did not consider it important, it went right out of my head.

There was the village council school and a higher-grade school in the village of Muirkirk three miles away. I just went to the village school. We played football in the playground, of course, and sometimes we got a game with another school, but we never had an organized school team. It was too small a school. If we played another school we managed to get some kind of strip together, but we played in our shoes.

When I left school I went to work at the pit, which was the usual thing in the village. I worked a section with my brother Bob for a time. Occasionally a boy would take a job on a farm, but we were not farm-minded people really.

There were plenty of mines, into which you could walk down an incline, and plenty of pits, where you had to go down by cage. There was no unemployment in the village at that time.

I went to a pit and spent the first six months working at the pit top. My wages would be no more than two shillings and sixpence a day. My job was to empty the trucks when they came up full of coal and send them back down the pit again and to sort out the stones from the coal on a conveyer-belt.

On Sunday you could make extra money emptying wagons of the fine coal we called dross, which was fed into about six big Lancashire boilers. You got sixpence a ton and each wagon contained maybe eight to ten tons. I've been in on a Sunday, just me and my shovel – as big as the wagon – and emptied two wagons, twenty tons, on my own. It was light stuff and nothing to us.

After about six months working at the pit top, a job that was active but not heavy, I went down to the pit bottom. The coal mines and pits were the first places to have electricity, before people had it in their houses, and the pit was like Piccadilly Circus. First I would shift full trucks and put them into the cages and then take out the empty trucks and run them along to where they were loaded. I did more running than lifting and at the end of an eight-hour shift I had probably run ten or twelve miles. This might have done me good – marathon-running!

Then I went into the back of the pit itself, where they were digging the coals and where they had the stables in which the ponies were kept. I felt sorry for the animals. When they were lowered down to the bottom of the pit, below the cage, it looked like cruelty, but it wasn't really. I've seen them in their stables, eating their straw. They could be there for months at a time. Then they took a break. They were blind then, but they recovered their sight. They used to pull a dozen of the trucks on the rails from the back end of the pit to the pit bottom.

At the back of the pit you realized what it was all about : the smell of damp, fungus all over the place, seams that had been worked out and had left big gaps, and the stench – not the best of air, though possibly better ventilated in mines and pits now. There was a ventilation system which diverted the air through channels with doors, canvas and all kinds of things. You were supposed to get air but I'm sure there were some places it did not reach. People got silicosis because they had no decent air to breathe.

In one part of the pit you went up an incline with the water gushing down it, and if the trucks went off the rails there, what an operation it was to put them back on again!

You would be down there eight hours and you would have your grub to eat there and a tea can wrapped up in a big, thick newspaper to keep it warm for a couple of hours, perhaps even less. You had to drink your tea maybe an hour after you'd started, otherwise it would probably be cold. You had to eat where you were working and there was no place to wash your hands. It was really primitive. The longest break you would get for anything would be half an hour, but if a man was digging coal on piece-work he could stop to eat anytime. If there were six men doing a job, three would take a break while three worked.

We would see a lot of rats in a mine, though not as many in a pit. In a mine the rats could go down the incline. But they did not frighten the men. Not at all. I have seen rats sitting on men's laps eating.

I went to the coal-face, but I didn't actually dig any coal. I was too young. I saw the firing of shots to bring down the coal – men boring the big holes, stabbing them up with powder or gelignite and then . . . whoof! And men putting up props before they could go in and waiting for the smoke to clear. A lot of men went in before the smoke had cleared, and they would get severe headaches.

We were filthy most of the time and never really clean. It was unbelievable how we survived. You could not clean all the parts of your body properly. Going home to wash in a tub was the biggest thing. The first time I was in a bath was when I was fifteen.

It was a terribly hard job and when I hear people castigating miners, saying they are too greedy, looking for too much money, I tell them they don't realize that long, long ago miners were trodden on. They are getting better wages now and better conditions. They have pit-head baths and can go home clean. But I have always had an affinity with the miner and I always will have.

There were a lot of accidents in the pits when the coal-cutting machines came. At first the men did not know how to work them properly. Those machines made a lot of noise and vibrated. I was lucky not to see any tragedies, because men were being killed all the time.

Whenever there is a mining disaster, all mining communities are affected by it. I remember the Gresford disaster in Wrexham in 1934, when 265 men died. The people in my village, and every other village in Britain, shared the grief of the people around Gresford.

I had become a football manager when there was a pit disaster in Muirkirk, the village next to Glenbuck. I knew quite a few of the men who died. If you have worked down the pit you tend to appreciate the better things in life and are keen to make the most of any opportunities that come your way.

After about two years in the pit I was unemployed. The old, old story. The pits closed. All of them. Men had to travel to other villages where the mines and pits were still working. I remember two men, James and Will McLatchie, who walked seven miles to a place appropriately called Coalburn, did a shift, and walked seven miles back. The pits started at seven o'clock in the morning, so if you were not at the pit-head then, when they started winding up coal, you didn't get down.

The pits never opened again in our village, but trains ran to other pits and men became commuters. They had to be up at five to go to the station four miles away. There would be three or four carriages with wooden seats and the train would run right close to the mine.

I signed on the dole. I don't remember how much money I drew each week, but it was very little. If I had any money I would have a game of cards. Otherwise I would go for long walks. There were no jobs, but my sister Liz had a newspaper round and I would go up to the station and help Liz deliver the papers in the village. I started doing this when I was at school and I helped again when I was out of work.

We took round morning papers and evening papers, and at night, when all was quiet, it could be a bit frightening. Some people wouldn't go down the lane at night, amongst the trees.

I would ride up to the houses on my bicycle, steady myself, and throw the papers. Sometimes I would walk into the houses and occasionally an old chap, who would be sitting in front of a fire, would give me an apple and perhaps a penny at weekends.

I was not unemployed for long, only a matter of months, before Carlisle United signed me. In the meantime I was playing junior football, and could earn five bob a game, or even seven shillings and sixpence. I had heard that Kilmarnock were interested in signing me, and I knew it would only be a matter of time before I became a professional player with one club or another. Even when I was in the pit I was only killing time – I had to make a living – until the time came when I would be playing football.

It was all worked out in my mind. I knew I had something to offer and I have always been an optimist. If I'd had to wait for a few years, it is possible that I might have lost my enthusiasm. But I was young and I felt that somewhere along the line I was being guided. I believed I had a destiny.

Life was not easy in the village when we were growing up. No disrespect to Glenbuck, but you would have been as far away from civilization in Outer Mongolia. The winters were cold and bitter, with four months of snow, and there was very little in the village so you had to go on long treks to get anything. The baker and the fruiterer used to come round in their vans from neighbouring villages until eventually they could not come because of the snow.

But we had a pair of shoes, maybe something to put on, maybe something to eat, though not always enough to fill us, and we had our pride and our characters, who made their own world, the best of a bad lot, the best of isolation. We listened to the wireless or read the papers, so we knew about Jarrow and what was happening to other miners. But we were cut off from the big cities, so we talked to each other and about each other. We had fun, jokes, laughs and exaggeration.

At school we were brought up on tales of Bruce, Wallace and Burns. They were the greatest. Our village was the greatest. Our school was the greatest. And the English were vilified. We thought England was our enemy and the English were poison.

Our conception of an Englishman was of someone who spoke differently from us, with a fancy dialect, plums in his mouth – 'I say, old chap,' and all that kind of stuff – with his coloured blazer and a white hankie in the breast pocket and his old school tie and straw hat and maybe some powder on his face. All Oxford and Noel Coward.

We seemed to forget about the miners in England, on Tyneside and in Yorkshire and Nottingham, who were just like us.

Later on, when I became an international footballer, I was like all Scots when confronted by England, the 'auld enemy'. We tend to revert to being savages for ninety minutes on those occasions. We become Wallace and Bruce and Sir James Douglas – the Black Douglas – when we put on the blue jersey. I've always wanted to win every game, but when I played for Scotland against England, the pride was there. Passion was always there when I played, but the pride was unbelievable.

I think the world of English people now – if anyone had told my father I would say that, he'd have shot me! – and I think they are the most tolerant people in the world. Having been amongst them for so long and having been accepted, I have tried to be a good citizen and consequently get a good name for Scottish people. Otherwise people might say, 'He's a bloody nuisance,' and when they came across other Scottish people they would say, 'Christ, they'll be the same as Bill Shankly!' By striving to do my best while living in England I hope I have compensated the English people for having suffered me!

Our village characters all had nicknames, like 'Barlinnie Swell', 'Wig', who had curly hair, 'Corry-Hughie', who was left-handed, and others like 'Snibs', 'Snooks', 'Lots', 'Pimp', 'Bird', 'Cob' and 'Bomber Brown'. My brother Jimmy was always 'Mickey' and I was 'Willie', pronounced 'Wullie'.

I used to mix with them in the pit and stand at the street corners at night, observing them and listening to their wonderful humour and exaggerated yarns, and this is where I picked up a lot of what I am. Where did Burns and Shakespeare and Wordsworth and men like those get their expressions from? From mixing with people.

After the pub had closed on Friday and Saturday nights we would stand near the sweet shop or chip shop or Co-operative shop. Those who hadn't been in the pub had been in the chip shop all night, eating, and drinking lemonade. We would stand there talking until the early hours of the morning.

Anybody who had a coat was a foreigner or a snob. We had jackets and open-neck shirts, even in the depths of winter. And the stories would start.

The humour was fantastic and nobody could master it better than my brother John. He could make a laugh out of any mortal thing. He could see something and turn it inside out. My brother Alec was a funny fellow too, very quick-witted.

The men would talk about the old-time football and how a fellow had a free kick at Kilmarnock one day and hit the bar and the ball bounced from one bar on to the other bar and went out of the ground, so that they had to throw in another ball! Sometimes the characters would bring along relatives who were well off or had perhaps been professional footballers, and they would show off. They would open their jackets to show you their waistcoats and medals and say, 'I got that one in the Boer War,' or 'I got that one for playing for Kilmarnock in the Scottish Cup Final,' and we would laugh.

The old man we called 'Bird', William Bone, told the most exaggerated yarns of all. He would tell how he was working down the pit pushing a truck full of coal and he pushed it three hundred yards before he realized it was off the rails, and how he had loaded three hundred trucks a day (when he had maybe loaded six). 'On Clydebank,' he would say, 'they had a big crane that used to lift the big boats out of the water and the men would hammer the bottoms of the boats and the crane would drop them back down again.' He was unbelievable, but quite serious.

We would stand or sit around listening. We all wore check cloth caps and would turn them upside down on our heads to signify we didn't believe him, and he would go mad and say, 'I'll bloody kill all of you!' But I'm sure if I had told a yarn about how I would go off to England and play for Preston in the Cup Final and for Scotland, and go to Liverpool and become King of the Kop, the men would have turned their caps upside down for me, too.

Drink was taboo – the curse of all. You would go to hell if you drank. That was you finished. That's how some people used to think. Old Scottish narrow-mindedness, if you like, and ridiculous, because anything in moderation is all right.

More than half the people in the village did not drink and only half of those who did drink would actually get drunk. When the men finished work on Fridays some of them would go to the pub and come out staggering. They would get drunk again on Saturday nights, sometimes paralytic. On Monday morning they would have no money and would be cadging sixpence to get a few cigarettes. They would work all week and then get drunk again on Friday and Saturday.

Some people go to a pub for company, a game of cards or darts or dominoes. But these men didn't go to the pub for that. They went to get drunk – really drunk. I've seen them drunk, and with four or five miles to walk. By the time they got home they were probably sober.

Some of the abstainers would see a man come out of the pub and say, 'Look at Alec Johnson,' or 'Look at Tom Smith,' or 'Look at Matt Park.' Matt was the character we called 'Lots', and he used to be a fair football player. 'Look at Matt,' they'd say. 'He's never sober. Isn't it terrible?'

I thought it was wrong to castigate a man who had been down the pit working in water all week because he felt like getting drunk at weekends. The people who stood around criticizing were the ones who made me sick. The men took a little drink, and being intoxicated with liquor, apparently, is a great feeling. I don't know because I have never been intoxicated like that. I have only been intoxicated with football. I was really intoxicated with elation the day I helped Preston win the Cup. I felt the way people probably feel when they've drunk two bottles of whisky.

Looking back, I can understand why some of the men drank a lot. There was not much for them to do, and after a week in the pit a man was entitled to his relaxation, whatever form it might take, as long as he did not harm others.

We were all gambling men, betting on horses and playing cards. When Sunday came along it was down to the woods, hiding away and playing pontoon. The law could have stopped us, of course, but we always knew where the village policeman was – and he knew where we were. There might be fifty at the card school but only a dozen actually playing. It took more than one to run the bank because we didn't have enough money and so used to club together and put the money in a cap. The first card was turned up, but the banker's card was turned down, and the bets went on. There was a limit on an ace. You couldn't put five pounds on an ace.

I saw twenty-pound bets when I was a boy, which was a lot of money for a man working in the pit – never mind Las Vegas!

You only backed the picture cards, but the men who were standing at the side or the back would bet on the cards of the men who were playing. They would watch the run, see who was doing well, and bet on those cards. Often the fellows at the back were winning and the fellows at the front were losing.

The games went on all day long and into the night, and boys would come to play from neighbouring villages. There was one from the village of Glespin whom we called 'Boss Marshall'. He was a good gambler and he would be handling five-pound notes

B

– the white ones – and pound notes and ten-shilling notes all day long. He would never bother to sort the notes out. He would just crush them and squeeze them until at the end of the day they were all crumpled up. We used to say, 'They'll have to be sent to be cleaned and pressed on Monday morning.'

I remember the men would be down on their haunches, in a squatting position, all day long. They were not uncomfortable because, as miners, they were used to working in that position.

It was pontoon on Sundays and brag the rest of the week. Strangers would have to be introduced by someone and they would be scrutinized. All eyes would be on them. Everyone lost money from time to time, but there was no trouble.

There were no cheats. If you had cheated, your life would have been in danger. Any hint of it and you would be asked to leave the school, never to return. If you lost you just walked away or borrowed five pounds, which is a bad way of gambling. If you are losing at cards you should get up and say, 'Sorry, boys, I'm cleaned out,' and off you go. If you borrow money to chase your losses you can get further into debt. Best just to leave. That way you will probably get over it in two days.

When I was a player at Preston I went home one Sunday in the summer. I was due to go to the Isle of Man for a holiday on the Monday, but on the Sunday night I got involved in a card school and lost all my money – sixty pounds – and couldn't go. The amazing part is that if I had won all the money in the school it would not have amounted to sixty pounds. I had the gambling bug when I was younger and I don't recommend it. It can be like a disease.

I'll never forget my first Sunday in Carlisle. I arrived on a hot August Saturday to play in a practice match. Tommy Curry, a truly wonderful man who later became trainer at Manchester United and lost his life in the Munich air disaster, was Carlisle's trainer then, and he had to play in the practice match to make up the team. I had not trained very much and that night I had cramp. It was so bad that I jumped out of bed into the middle of the floor.

I was tired and on my own, so on the Sunday I went to the

ground to see if there was enough hot water to have a bath. There was a bunch of players in a card school, fellows from all over England who had been with big clubs and were on the way down. I joined in their game, but they were not the kind of men I was used to playing against at home. I felt there was some kind of fiddling going on. Two players can put one out of business at cards and I felt this was happening. But that didn't deter me and when I left the ground at lunchtime I didn't have a penny. And that's how I spent my first Sunday night in Carlisle, walking round the place, completely broke.

Next morning I told Tommy Curry I was cleaned out and he gave me a couple of shillings and said, 'Oh you shouldn't play with them – they clean me out every time I go.' This was true, because I remember every time Tommy would go to play cards he would smile and say, 'I'll go down and give them a donation!'

Footballers play cards a lot – they spend so much time travelling and staying at hotels. It can be a good thing as long as they don't overdo it, but I think it can be bad for them to play cards for money just before they are going to play a match. If you go to the races and lose a hundred pounds you get over it in a couple of days, and it is the same with cards. But if you lose money on the way to a match you feel terrible and it will upset your game, because there is not enough time to get over it.

I've known players lose twenty pounds before a game, and twenty pounds before the war was a lot of money. I've seen players skinned like that and I've helped them out with a loan. They would pay me on a Monday, perhaps – and then be back again the next Monday. Some players have been in debt up to their eyeballs and I have heard of one boy in recent years who even had to re-mortgage his house because of gambling debts.

Football managers have got to keep an eye on the card schools before matches to see that they don't get out of hand. If they do, then a manager should step in and limit them. Some players can gamble and it does not affect their play at all. Stan Bowles, of Queen's Park Rangers, has had a lot of publicity about his gambling problem. On the whole it might not affect Stan's play, but if he lost a lot of money before a big match it possibly would affect him. I'm sure it would have affected me if I had gambled heavily before a big match.

In the village, apart from the yarns and the cards, we had the pictures in Muirkirk and football of course. Going to the pictures was a bonus for us, living where we lived. We would walk through the snow and the rain to go to the cinema.

I remember the silent films, when there would be a piano playing in the cinema and sometimes even an orchestra. When you see those films now they look really comical. And then there was Al Jolson in *The Singing Fool*. The cinema at Muirkirk took about six hours to show it – the film broke down about forty times and ran until three o'clock in the morning.

Later on there were John and Lionel Barrymore, who were brilliant, and W. C. Fields and Jack Holt and James Cagney and Humphrey Bogart and Spencer Tracy and Clark Gable. I don't think Gable was a natural actor but he would always get the big parts. He always had a kind of cocky look about him, like good boxers and footballers. He would aggravate you. He was the big man. When he came into a room people would stand up.

I loved the Westerns – the Younger Brothers and Jesse James. In *The Great Missouri Raid* they all joined forces, to raid all the banks in their long white coats.

When the talkies started there were marvellous gangster films with all the jargon – 'coitens' and 'moider' and 'take you for a ride' and 'put you in a wooden overcoat.' The mobsters used to walk about with their bodyguards around them, all wearing grey suits with long jackets, wide lapels and padded shoulders.

There would always be a 'wise guy' who would say to one of the other gangsters, a stooge, like Warren Hymer, 'That's a beautiful suit you've got on.'

'Do you think so, boss?'

'Yeah – whose is it?'

There were films about Al Capone, true stories, and violence. But I don't believe films like these make people want to go out and shoot other people. You are only a rogue if you are born

a rogue. Nobody makes you one. You might be led astray sometimes to do something stupid, but in the end it's up to you. Nobody makes you a criminal unless you want to be one. Nobody
forces you to take dope unless you want to take it.

The whole area around where we lived was laced with junior
football teams. If you had gone into any village in Scotland
with a ball and asked any boy to take it, I'd bet he would be
a good kicker of a football.

Our village team was Glenbuck Cherrypickers, but the club
was near extinction when I had a trial at sixteen, and I never
actually played for them. I was a bit young for the Cherrypickers, who were in the Ayrshire League, a hard league, and
preferred experienced men. It was the club's last season anyway,
and the next season I played half a season for Cronberry, which
was about twelve miles from where I lived.

I used to cycle to the ground, play the game, and cycle back.
When we played away matches we would travel by charabanc
or train. After half a season I went to Carlisle United, but I
learnt a lot from Scottish junior football and from watching and
listening to players, especially my brothers.

Today all the top clubs have apprentice players who are
looked after in every way and play against boys their own age
and have coaches to train them. But in the old days we were
thrown in amongst men, against old-timers who knew what the
game was all about. It was hard, but if you survived it you were
a player ready for anything. So few great players are coming
through today's system that I think we got more results from the
way we did it in the old days.

Football is a highly specialized profession. A great player will
be a great player in any club at any time. But a lot of good
players have got into the wrong hands and have been brought
up the wrong way.

Often at Liverpool I would offer words of encouragement to
boys on the way up, but when they were pulling on their jersey
to play for the first team I would say, 'The fun's finished now.
You're playing for Liverpool. You're playing for a living now.'

I have handled dozens and dozens of men of different temperaments. As a player I knew I was going to make it with or without an apprentice scheme. Players like Tommy Finney and Tommy Docherty knew it too, and it was obvious to me as a manager at Liverpool that players like Ian Callaghan, Tommy Smith, Chris Lawler and Phil Thompson were going to make it.

When I saw young Phil I decided he had tossed up with a sparrow for his legs and lost. He was not the strongest boy in the world, but he had heart. The ability was there, plus the ambition and the passion, the will to win. Thompson, Callaghan, Smith, Lawler and others all had these qualities and would have made it whether they had come through an apprentice scheme, junior football or the Lancashire Combination. A hard upbringing in football can help. The soft stuff will never help.

When I played in Scotland they called it junior football, but it was junior in name only. There was no age limit and it was a hard school, filled with experienced professionals.

You learn more from your mistakes than from anything else. Instead of being told, 'Hard lines, son,' and that kind of stuff, and having to listen to all the fancy talk which is sometimes difficult to assimilate, you were told to 'justify your inclusion.' Harsh words – but if you had the character to overcome that system and fend for yourself, that was survival.

I remember going home from Preston to referee a game of junior football all-stars. Cronberry had a fellow called Fred Standring, whose brother, Stanley, had been a great old player for the club at one time. Fred was a dribbler, and he'd been dribbling about and losing the ball. Stanley had been watching, and at half-time he said to Fred, 'Listen, if I'd an arm the length of the pitch I'd have knocked your bloody head off.'

That was typical of the no-nonsense approach that was hard to take but produced real players, like Bobby Collins, who went straight into Celtic's team from junior football.

All the teams had men who could handle themselves, and there was a certain amount of protection for boys of sixteen or seventeen. The older players wouldn't stand by and see a boy kicked around. You would be playing against lions, but there would be lions on your side as well.

There were a lot of hard men about. When I was a boy a junior team came to play in Glenbuck and brought a crowd of hooligans with them on a special train to cause trouble and disrupt the game and help them win it that way. They started a fight – oh, what a brawl it was! – and my brother Alec was in it. Men were belting each other against barbed wire. There were a few broken noses that day.

The information I picked up from Alec, Jimmy, Bob and John was invaluable. I saw them play and I played with them, and they could do cunning and crafty things. Alec loved to play and he was a great psychologist too. He could not show you how to play, but he could help you because he knew the ins and outs of the game and what made people tick on a football field. He could give advice, and the advice he gave me was the best I ever had. He said, 'Don't ever try and argue with the referee. I've been at it all my life and where does it get you? He always wins in the end.'

That does not seem very much, but it was possibly responsible for Preston winning the FA Cup. All the players were running around shouting at the referee, but I said, 'Oh, you're right, referee. We were wrong.' And I'm not the calmest of people if I'm fighting for my life or fighting to win a football match – I would die for that! But I had enough sense not to aggravate referees. I had enough sense to heed the advice of my brother Alec.

Don't get frustrated when a foul is given against you. Get back and stop it from resulting in a goal. The referee will not change his mind, so you are wasting energy and time, that's all. If you argue with him you get upset, you're not normal, and you are likely to do something stupid. The system is against you. If you try and tell a referee what to do he'll resent it and think, 'What the hell are you talking about?'

Right from the start I'd say to him, 'Well done, ref, you're right. It was a good decision.' I carried this right through my playing career and passed on Alec's advice to the players at the clubs where I became manager.

I always lived up to it – except once. I broke the rule when I was the manager of Liverpool and we were in the Second Division. Only the captain could appeal to referees but we were having so many goals disallowed that I decided to see the referee before each match and say, 'We don't want to badger you by appealing because it's against the laws, but if the captain is up here and something happens way down there, he can't appeal to you. I would ask you if our nearest player to you could appeal. Nobody else will come. We won't flood you. But if we think it is something blatant, will you accept an appeal from the nearest player?'

To my mind, what we were trying to do would help the game and help the referee. But six managers out of ten usually have something in mind to benefit themselves, and the referees treated me the same as them. They thought I was trying to con them when really I was just being straight with them. That season we won the Second Division championship hands down, but we must have had sixteen goals disallowed.

It was nonsense, so before the season was over I changed my philosophy for a while. Turning the other cheek did not get us anywhere, so I told my players: 'If you think a decision is wrong, storm up to the referee and surround him, every one of you. Make his life rough.'

I had players who would have appealed against anything, and they had been held back. They had been good little boys. I told them to start protesting. I said. 'This "Yes, sir, no, sir, three bags full, sir" stuff is getting us nowhere, so if there is a penalty awarded against us or anything like that, march round about the referee and complain about it.'

The worst decision of the lot that season was at Newcastle. We were winning 2–0 and Ian St John smashed one into the net – and the referee gave a foul for us! A goal then would have finished the game, but later we missed a penalty and Newcastle scored to make it 2–1.

Even when we decided to swarm around the referee we still had goals disallowed. Alec was right. The referee always wins in the end. Before the last war refereeing was a little different. You could have a chat with them and maybe even shout at them and they would shout back, 'Same to you!' Some referees will do that today and, to be fair, the refereeing I have seen recently has been good.

As a player I specialized in tackling, which is an art, and I was never sent off the field or had my name in a referee's book. The art of tackling, as with many things, is in the timing – the contact, winning the ball, upsetting the opposition, maybe even hurting them. You're in, you're out, you've won it and you've hurt him and left him lying there, but it's not a foul because you have timed everything right.

I played it hard but fair. No cheating. I'd have broken somebody's leg maybe, with a hard tackle, with a bit of spirit, but that's a different story from cheating. Cheats will always be caught in the finish. Punishment is sometimes a long time coming, but it comes. If you've done something really vile, you will be caught in the end.

There was one player I remember who, from the age of sixteen built himself up as football's answer to Billy the Kid. Joe Mercer, for one, will know who I'm referring to. This fellow had all the dirty tricks in the trade. He would catch people in the windpipe with an elbow, kick at ankles, take a swipe at heads when he could. You name it, he did it.

He got me in the diaphragm and really sickened me, so I joined the growing number of players with scars on their bodies who were looking for him. There were people who would have crippled him. It was like turning an army against himself. He got away with it for a long, long time, but he got what was coming to him in the end.

I hurt him myself in one game – and he was hurt a few times before he was finished. I got him in a tackle. It looked legitimate, but it wasn't. If you're a good tackler you can hurt people, and I made sure I got him. He was finished for that day. He was being repaid by player after player and in the end he got a bad injury.

When I was brought up in Scotland you were either one thing or the other, Protestant or Catholic, which also meant Rangers or Celtic – and whichever you were, the other people were wrong. That was the atmosphere, but I've been in England for forty-three years and I've learnt to think differently. Fortunately there is nothing like the Rangers-Celtic situation in Liverpool. The supporters of Liverpool and Everton are a mixed bunch. The only religion talked about is football.

I was brought up as a Presbyterian, Church of Scotland. I went to Sunday school and I received a bible for perfect attendance in one year. I still have that bible. My mother was a religious woman, a Christian if ever one was born, but she did not go to church every Sunday because she couldn't afford the time to go. She had the dinner to make, for as many as you get in a restaurant every day. She had no bigotry and latterly, when she had only John staying with her, a young chap called Bill Smith, one of the Plymouth Brethren, used to go to see her every night and read to her from the Bible. Bill was killed in the Muirkirk pit disaster.

My father didn't go to church, but he was an honest man, which to me made him religious. I have my own beliefs and I don't have an axe to grind against anyone else's religious beliefs. That's their business.

During my career as a player I played alongside boys of different religions. There have been cases, I'm sure, where boys have not been picked for a team because they were a certain religion, but that would never influence me. At Liverpool, for instance, all the staff – the office staff, the training staff and the players – had their own religions, but that didn't make any difference.

People are entitled to their own religious beliefs and their own politics. I'm a socialist, though I do not have any great faith in any of the political parties. The socialism I believe in is not really politics. It is a way of living. It is humanity. I believe the only way to live and to be truly successful is by collective effort, with everyone working for each other, everyone helping each other, and everyone having a share of the rewards at the end of the day. That might be asking a lot, but it's the way I see football and the way I see life.

If somebody gave me something when I was a boy I used to say, 'Oh, good God, is it true – are you joking?' When you have very little you tend to appreciate things. I appreciated things then and I appreciate anything that is ever done for me now.

Of the people we were brought up to idolize – Wallace, Bruce and Burns – the greatest to us was Robert Burns, who was born twenty-six miles from our village, in Alloway, Ayr. The things he wrote are unbelievable considering he lived for so short a time.

Burns quoted the ranks – 'A man's a man for a' that' – and laced into the big people, the lords. He murdered those kind of people. 'He struts and stares about' – he owns an estate and you have to work for him – 'while hundreds worshipped at his word' – doing exactly what he told them. 'He's but a quiff' – a nincompoop. He's nothing.

It was not hard for us to grow fond of a person who saw things that way. It was possibly a good atmosphere in which to be brought up, inasmuch as there was a lot of honesty: in my brothers and sisters, my father, and of course my mother.

She achieved a miracle of dedication. I try, but mine is nothing in comparison with hers.

2 The Road South

I was recommended to Carlisle United by a scout, Peter Carruthers, who lived not far from Glenbuck in the village of Kirkconnell. My last game for Cronberry was at Sanquhar, Dumfries-shire. Mr Carruthers saw me in that match and recommended me to Carlisle for a month's trial. I would have been just over seventeen years old.

It was the first time I had been out of Scotland. I had been to Glasgow to see Rangers and Celtic – that was the ultimate – and to Motherwell, Hamilton, Ayr and Kilmarnock to see games, but never further than that. The standard of football in Scotland then was as high as ever, and I would have been happy to have signed for a team up there. But I got the chance to come to play in England and I didn't want to give up the opportunity.

My brother Alec went down to Carlisle with me. It was the week before the season opened and they were short of players, but they had a practice match for me to play in and Tommy Curry played to make up the numbers.

All I wanted was a chance and Carlisle came along and offered me the trial, which wasn't very satisfactory because if I hadn't played well I'd have been thrown on the scrap-heap. I'd have had to have gone back home and started again. But it was an opportunity to show my ability and after I'd played one game for them the trial was finished. It was against Middlesbrough reserves, who gave us an awful tanking. They beat us 6–0 and it was real torture, but I must have done enough to justify myself, because I signed for Carlisle after that one game.

Carlisle were in the Third Division (North) and the reserves played in the North Eastern League, which was a very good league. Middlesbrough played a tremendous brand of football, rolling the ball about. Charlie Ferguson, who became Sunderland's chief scout, was playing for Middlesbrough when I had that trial game. My next game was at Jarrow, the famous Jarrow. It was hard going in the North Eastern League.

The manager of Carlisle then was Billy Hampson, a quiet, sensible man who later became manager of Leeds United. He picked his games for me. The team wasn't great, so he thought, 'You're not going to get mangled in there.' He would take me to one side and say, 'We're playing away to Rotherham. That's not for you.'

At the end of the season we won the North Eastern League Cup, a trophy Newcastle United reserves had never won. And we beat them 1–0 in the final. I've still got the medal.

Most of the players at Carlisle had been with big clubs, Tottenham or Newcastle or West Ham, clubs like those. It was full of Tynesiders and Scottish players. Every team had a load of them in those days: useful players, old stagers.

Johnny Kelly was the goalkeeper. He came from Celtic, and was a bit of a boxer as well. He once sparred with Tommy Milligan, the middleweight champion of Britain – and one day, in a match, he put an opposing player on the floor. He just panned him and down he went, so Kelly walked off the field after that. He sent himself off!

I was in digs with Johnny and a fellow called Bob Bradley, the right back and captain, a Tynesider who had been on the books of one of the London clubs. They helped me too. We lived two or three minutes' walk from the ground and we were all cheery chaps who enjoyed a good singsong round a piano. The fellows were always neat and clean, well groomed. They went to the barber regularly – and not the ladies' hairdresser – and kept their shoes well polished and were a good example to everybody.

I was never homesick, but I think if you are ambitious the place you go to doesn't make any difference. I was ambitious – impatient, if you like, because ambition is a form of impatience. You want to get at something before it's there. You want to burst the balloon before it's blown up.

There were only two things for me at Carlisle, the football ground and the football. I had an uncle, Billy Blyth, my mother's brother, on the board of directors at Carlisle, and he had a pub. I used to go and see him occasionally and he was a nice man who gave me a lot of good advice. But my playing had nothing to do with my uncle. If you had ten uncles on the board and couldn't play you wouldn't get a chance. You'd get humped out.

I could go home from Carlisle for twelve shillings then, and I would go every other weekend. But that was secondary. Carlisle was only a stepping-stone. I knew I was going further than that. I was there for one season and I learned a lot from Tommy Curry, the trainer, and Billy Hampson and Uncle Billy and Johnny Kelly and Bob Bradley.

At the end of the season I was paid four pounds ten shillings a week, which was good, because the top rate in English football then was eight pounds. I was much better off than the coal-miner for doing something in the fresh air that I would have done for nothing.

3 Change at Haltwhistle

At the end of the season at Carlisle I was on my way home for the summer half an hour after the last whistle.

The boys who worked in the pit finished at about two or two-thirty in the afternoon and, after they had eaten, the card games would start – brag or pontoon, usually brag during the week. A penny to blind and twopence to brag.

We were sitting on the football pitch, which was across the road from our house. My brother Bob was there, I think. And one of my sisters, I can't remember which, came over and said, 'There's a telegram for you.' That caused a commotion. I opened it, and it was from Carlisle: 'TRAVEL TO CARLISLE TOMORROW STOP CARLISLE UNITED.'

So we contacted Carlisle and found out that another club was after me, and I travelled down again, with my brother Alec, who had accompanied me when I went for the trial. We went to my Uncle Billy's and he said Preston were after me and told me to see Bill Scott, who was then Preston's trainer and later became the supervisor and manager, before going to Sunderland.

I asked Uncle Billy what the fee was and he said five hundred pounds, of which I would get forty-five or fifty pounds plus a ten-pound signing-on fee, and wages of five pounds a week. I said, 'If things are dearer at Preston I'm going to be out of pocket.'

I was quite happy at Carlisle because I had visions of playing in the team the whole time the next season. I'd be about eighteen then. Preston were struggling in the Second Division. They had just escaped relegation and bought one or two old players. They bought Bob Kelly, the great English international, who was forty-two years old then. I have never seen anybody so quick over twenty yards at his age. He was small and fit, a forward who could score goals from outside the penalty box. They had Dick Rowley, a big inside left who was an Irish international and whose father was the manager of the greyhound track at Preston. And there was goalkeeper Harry Holdcroft, from Everton, who had class and played for England.

They thought they had a good team and could get promotion. Bill Scott was giving us this tale. And I said, 'No, it's not worth going. Forty pounds? I could win that at pontoon on a Sunday – or I could lose it. And ten bob a week more wages? I'm not getting anything out of it.'

So Bill Scott went off to the station on his way to New-castle to sign another player, so he said. Actually I think he was going home to Sunderland. Then my brother Alec started talking to me. 'It's not what you're going to get now, it's what you're going to get later,' he said. 'It's opportunity. Preston's a bigger club. They used to be a great team and they might be again.'

We decided to rush to the station and we just caught Bill Scott as he was going on to the train. I signed on in a carriage, got my ten pounds signing bonus on the train, and got off again at Haltwhistle and caught a train back to Carlisle. Not going to Preston was as close as that.

I reported to Preston in July 1933, but if I hadn't moved there it would only have been a matter of time before somebody else would have picked me up, I'm sure of that. Newcastle would have signed me, no danger, because I was on their doorstep and had played in the North Eastern League against their reserve team.

If you can play you will make it eventually, but there were hundreds of players then. All the mining areas had players and there were a lot of professionals who hadn't made the grade and the clubs couldn't afford to pay them. There was the same kind of pessimism as you hear now – 'The game's going to go,' and all that – but it was worse then. Hundreds of boys who had been away and had maybe done a season at Tottenham or Sheffield United or Derby County, were on the scrap-heap, playing in the Third Division (North) for a fiver a week. And there was a lot of unemployment.

Five pounds was reasonable money then, but some of the Southern clubs in the Third Division were paying eight pounds a week. My brother Jimmy got that at Southend – the same money as Hughie Gallacher got for playing for Newcastle United.

So, as my brother Alec pointed out, going to Preston was an opportunity for me. I was in my teens when I started playing in the team at right half.

When I arrived at Preston there was no manager. Bill Scott was the head trainer, supervisor and liaison man with the directors. The chairman, Mr James (J. I.) Taylor, was the managing director and he ran the club. He had never played, but he was a shrewd man who knew the game and he came to the ground every day, despite business commitments.

The board would pick the team, with Bill Scott and his assistant trainer, Jim Metcalfe. But James Taylor would have most say in this.

I started off in the Central League team and my first game was against Blackpool on the opening day of the season. It was warm and I had my hair shorn off in those days – like Kojak – because it was cleaner that way and I didn't have to go to the barbers so often. My opponent that day was Bobby Finan, who played for years at Blackpool and scored hundreds of goals. I remember the game well. Bobby and I were making our debuts and we spoke to each other.

We beat Blackpool reserves at home that day, and it was an especially good result considering we lost a player because of a broken leg – a close friend, Joe Brain, a Welsh boy who played centre forward. Big Louis Cardwell hurt Joe Brain in a tackle, and that was a blow for Joe because he was shaping to become a brilliant player. He was never the same player afterwards. We

were always together around Preston. He was a wonderfully
funny chap, with good patter, and he could sing too.

Our reserve team was a mixture of old players and inexperienced players. One day, in late October or early November, we
played Birmingham City reserves at Preston and beat them by
a big score. Freddie Harris, an inside forward with Birmingham,
asked me, 'Have you not played any League football yet?' and
I said 'No.' That was all Freddie said, but Jim Metcalfe must
have been pushing me, because the next week I was in the first
team.

That game was against Hull City (I've still got my player's
tickets for ten full peace-time seasons at Preston and know every
match I played in) and they had men like big Jack Hill in their
team. Hull had been promoted from the Third Division (North)
and it was ironical because I had played against them the year
before when I was at Carlisle, and they had murdered us 6–1 at
Hull.

They had played offside tactics, with their players all backed
up to the halfway line, and nobody could defeat them. And
they had a fellow called Sergeant, who played outside left, a good
player. I had played against them as a boy and now I was old
enough in the head to think. I broke through early on and it
resulted in a goal and we won 5–0.

Imagine losing 6–1 against Hull and then beating them 5–0
in your next game against them! I caused a little bit of trouble
because I knew their tactics, and I said to Sergeant, 'It's a
different story today, son.'

Preston went on to win promotion as runners-up to Grimsby
Town in the Second Division in my first season in the team and
my wages were raised to eight pounds (six pounds in the summer).
Maybe I should make no comment, but the season I went to
Preston they were promoted to the First Division and when I
left, in 1949, they were relegated. I had ten full seasons with the
club in peacetime, but there were six years of the war, so I was
connected with Preston for sixteen years altogther.

We more than held our own in the First Division. We were
very steady, and if anyone had said, 'North End have lost two

goals,' nobody would have believed it. Arsenal were the kings in the 1930s of course. They had everything, the marble halls of Highbury, and aluminium massage baths. Their players walked about the dressing-rooms wearing white hooded robes, the way Muhammad Ali does today. Arsenal thought big.

The highlights for Preston were the successive FA Cup Finals, losing in 1937 and winning in 1938. Sunderland had won the League championship in 1936 and were then the best team I had played against. They were a free-running, attacking team and made full use of space on the field. Even their full backs, Jimmy Gorman and Alec Hall, attacked you – and this was in the days when all teams had wingers of course. They had two wonderful inside forwards, the great Raich Carter, at inside right, and Patsy Gallacher, who played directly against me in the Final and who scored sixteen goals with his head one season. That team was so good that it was a frightening experience to go to Roker Park.

Sunderland were a better team in 1936 than when they beat us 3–1 in the 1937 Final, but they were still better than Preston on the day at Wembley. We had beaten them in the league at Preston that season. Our goalkeeper, Harry Holdcroft, was injured and missed the Final, and Mick Burns, whom Preston signed from Newcastle, took his place. With no disrespect to Mick, I believe we would have had a better chance if Harry, who was so much a part of our team, had been able to play.

If we had reversed a 3–1 defeat by Arsenal in a League match at Deepdale towards the end of the 1937–38 season, we would have won the League and FA Cup double. Instead, Arsenal won the championship, Wolves were runners-up, and we were third.

To underline the strength and attitude of our club that season, on Saturday, 9 April 1938, four of the players – Andy Beattie, Tommy Smith, George Mutch and myself – represented Scotland against England at Wembley and Preston went ahead with a home League game against Derby County on the same day. Scotland beat England 1–0 and Preston beat Derby 4–1.

But we did beat Arsenal – Ted Drake, George Male, Eddie

Hapgood, and all of them – in the sixth round of the FA Cup on our way back to Wembley in 1938.

James Taylor, our chairman, was a tremendous character – alive, lucid, clever, cunning, devious and sarcastic. After that match at Highbury, Sir Frederick Wall, who was the big man at Arsenal then, came into the dressing-room wearing an astrakhan coat down to his feet, and I said, 'Oh, Christ, it's Methuselah!' We were all doubled up and James Taylor came in and said to Sir Frederick and anybody else within hearing distance, 'You know, it's a shame. It's not right that a little village team can come down here and beat Arsenal. It's wrong. They shouldn't do that.'

That was real sarcasm, salt into the wound. It was Taylor at his brilliant best. When Sunderland beat us 3–1 at Wembley in 1937, he had stood up and had said we'd be back again. He was crying, shedding big tears of disappointment. So we went back the next year and we beat Huddersfield Town 1–0. And James went to the town hall and got a big reception.

He could have been prime minister. His brain was so alert and he was so witty. But witty people can be sarcastic. When we were beaten he would have a few drinks and keep us waiting for about twenty minutes on the bus. Then he would arrive, with his bowler-hat and cravat, and he would turn to one of the players, perhaps goalkeeper Harry Holdcroft, and say, 'That last goal, Harry. It wasn't fair. I saw what happened. Just as you were about to dive for the ball the crowd at the back of the goal pushed the bloody ground. I saw them.'

You could learn from James Taylor, but some of the things he did were wrong, so later in life I would do the opposite. He would maybe be waiting for someone, Bill Scott for instance, and he'd shout, 'Scott!' He wouldn't call him by his first name, and everyone could feel it, the dagger bit. But Bill would say, 'Listen, you, I've got a handle to my jug. Don't you call me Scott again.' Scott would put him in his place, and Taylor would appreciate that.

Of all the things that can happen in the game, when the whistle blows at Wembley and you've played in a Final and you've won, that's the greatest thrill of your life as a player. No doubt about that. I thanked God for that. The feeling is unbelievable.

It was a big thrill to play for Scotland, and to captain them during the war was a proud moment. But to win the FA Cup was a different thing altogether. I played in three Finals, including the 1941 war Cup Final, when we went to Wembley with Tom Finney and a bunch of boys to play Arsenal.

We were champions of the North and Arsenal were champions of the South and we drew with them at Wembley and beat them at Blackburn the next week. OK the war was on, but it was still a Cup Final and we eventually beat them. So we gave Arsenal some digs in the ribs.

The 1938 Final was not a good game. Wembley was dry at the end of the season and the grass was shorn. I'd played for Scotland there two weeks earlier when we'd beaten England and the grass was too short, bad for playing. They ought to have let it grow a bit to have deadened the ball and to have slowed the game down. But the ball was shooting off the pitch.

The match was settled when George Mutch scored the only goal with a penalty right at the end of extra time. He just put the ball down on the spot, kept his eye on it and belted it. The ball hit the bar, which was square then, took the paint off it, screamed into the middle of the goal and ran down the back of the net. (The paint is on the ball to this day. I saw it again in 1971, when Liverpool reached the Final and played Arsenal. When we were preparing for Wembley, Tommy Smith, who was the Preston captain in 1938, came to the training ground at Melwood and showed the ball to his namesake, Tommy Smith, the Liverpool captain in 1971.)

I had run up from the back in case there was a rebound and I was the first to reach Mutch. I picked him up and lifted him above my head. He knew it was in. Then Huddersfield kicked off. I think Andy Beattie was the last to kick the ball, and he kicked it into the crowd and that was it. The whistle blew for time up.

What I remember best are the scenes when we had been up to the royal box and received our medals. We were back on the track near the pitch and the band played the National Anthem. Alf Young, the Huddersfield centre-half, who had conceded the penalty, was crying. A big strong man, crying. Alf was not crying because he was soft. He was crying with emotion, because he felt he had been responsible for losing the Cup. He had tackled George Mutch and as a result Mutch had scored from the penalty spot. It was warm and the Preston players posed for photographers. Tommy Smith, the captain, was carried shoulder-high and we all had our hands on the Cup. The sweat poured off us, even though we had short-sleeved jerseys, having learned from the year before. I've still got that silk jersey, made in Preston.

Around this time I saw Tommy Finney with number ten on his back playing for Preston schoolboys. It was obvious he could play, even then, when he was only a little boy. He started at the club during the war and was brought into the team for the regional games. Then he played his first game at Wembley in the 1941 wartime Cup Final. Eddie Hapgood was up against him and they were saying down there in London, 'Good God, what's this we've got?' Tommy was a riot. He was brilliant.

I played behind Tommy until I went into the RAF. Then Tommy went into the Army and signed as a professional after the war. I then played a couple of seasons with him. You could find him with your eyes shut. He always positioned himself so that he was easy to find. Lying deep, if the ball came across, you'd hook it with your left foot and you knew Tommy would pick it up.

He preferred to play on the right, but he could play anywhere. He could play wing half, he could play midfield – Tommy would have been the best midfield player in the world – and he could take the ball off the strongest of men.

Dribbling was a gift he had. He was naturally left-footed and did all his manipulating with his left, but he was useful with both feet and could shoot and head the ball. And, despite all this, he'd be round the back of the stand at Deepdale working on his game.

The base of the stand, the 'scratching pen', was concrete, and Tommy used to take the ball and lace it against the concrete, take it with his left foot, dribble a little bit, play it back against the wall, take it in his stride on his right foot, like taking a pass, dribble, and so on. Tommy Finney, with all his skills, was out there practising an elementary thing. But it was this dedication, allied to his skill and speed off the mark, that made Tommy such a formidable player.

There were always comparisons between Tommy and Stan Matthews. Stan played outside right of course. That's where he always played. Tommy could play anywhere. But Stan was a great player. Oh, what a brilliant player! He had tremendous pace and trickery. He could wriggle out through the eye of a needle. And he was a very fit fellow, a great credit to the game.

If you had been picking a team you could have played both Tommy and Stan because you could have put Stan at outside right and have given Tommy any position. After outside right, Tommy preferred to play centre forward. He was a good centre forward because he was good in the air. He could time his jumping and cause trouble.

Tommy never complained if ever he was hurt in tackles. He probably hurt quite a few people in the tackles too, but he had a lot of injuries, straining muscles, because of his acceleration. He was like Victor Sylvester – quick-quick-slow – only Tommy had a ball. If Victor Sylvester had a ball he'd probably fall on his backside.

No one can take anything away from Stan. He could run like a whippet. He could carry the ball thirty, forty, fifty, sixty yards and you couldn't take it off him. Tom could do those things too, and Tom gave more direct passes for you to have a shot at goal. Stan had more speculative lobs. Tommy would go to the byline and say, 'Come on, son,' with his finger. 'There you are – have a shot at that one.'

Andy McLaren came to Preston and Tommy used to roll passes back to him with both feet. One day, in a wartime regional league match, McLaren scored six goals from six cut-backs side-footed by Tommy, who was a menace. Many times when Tommy had the ball his right foot would be over the byline and he would poke the ball back with his left.

At Leeds one day – it was the season Leeds went down right after the war – Tommy turned them inside out. He had the goalkeeper demented, not knowing whether Tommy was going to cut the ball back or cross it. Tommy rolled a couple into the net. He had the goalkeeper out of his goal so much that in the end Tommy just put the ball on the left foot and put it inside the near post himself.

Tommy tore Derby County apart in a match shortly after the war. The pitch was a quagmire, but the mud didn't hinder Tommy at all. He trailed the ball past opponents, cut it across the penalty area, won free kicks and penalty kicks and made Derby wish he was a million miles away. It was one of the most remarkable games I can remember, because we won 7–4 and I scored three goals in a game for the only time in my career.

I scored a goal from a free kick, another from a penalty, and the third was a bit of a fluke. I chipped the ball and it rolled into the net. I scored two penalties in the wartime Cup semi-final against Newcastle, but that game against Derby at Preston was the only time I scored three. Raich Carter was with Derby then, and so was little Billy Steele, a great inside forward from Scotland. Angus Morrison, a big centre-forward, also scored three goals, and Preston signed him after that match.

Tommy was injured regularly, and when he was a boy the other players in the team used to look after him a bit in matches. I remember playing in one game when an experienced Scottish player threatened Tommy. He said, 'I'll break your leg.' I heard this, so I went over to the player and I told him, 'Listen, you break his leg and I'll break yours. Then we'll both be finished, because I'll get sent off.' He didn't bother Tommy after that.

Tommy was always a civil boy, courteous to everyone. I wouldn't say he cracked jokes in the dressing-room, but he didn't have to. We had enough comedians. We could laugh because we knew Tommy was on our side.

I once took the ball off Stan Matthews in a match and I got a big cheer for doing that. You always got a big cheer if you took the ball off Stan, but what I did was not particularly clever. I was at right half and Stan was on the opposite side of the field.

But when he had the ball I went across the pitch. He always held on to the ball, and I just anticipated how he would beat an opponent and then I nipped the ball off him. Standing behind someone else and anticipating moves – a two-against-one situation – was something we practised at Preston. Taking the ball off a player who has just beaten someone else is like stealing.

A boy called Kenny Horton, who works for Tommy now, took my position at right half in the Preston team. I was brought back for a spell, then Horton took over again. Shortly after I left the club, Tommy Docherty came in.

I wrote to Tommy Docherty when he played for Preston and said, 'Now you've got that jersey on, let it run about. It will guide you. It will take you round, no danger.' He was worth his weight in gold, a hard boy who had a big heart and never shirked a tackle. I wouldn't have minded four or five Tommy Dochertys in my team. You could depend on him to give you your money's worth. Tommy was like me in build, accent and attitude on the field. I wrote to him again when he played for Scotland, and he went on to get more caps than me of course.

It was always one of my big ambitions to play for Scotland and I wondered for a while if the fact that I was playing for an English club would be detrimental to my international chances. In those days, if it was a touch-and-go choice between two players, one who was playing in Scotland and the other in England, the selectors would go for the boy back home.

At Preston I was with a club that was small in comparison to some others, but I was in a good team, a team that played with intelligence, and I was more than holding my own against English international players. I felt that the Scottish selectors would have to take notice of me, and I have an idea that the Preston chairman, James Taylor, was pushing my name forward whenever he could.

Andy Beattie, who played behind me in the Preston team and who was to play such an important part in my football career, as you will discover later, was selected before I was. That was in 1937, and I remember going to Andy's digs to congratulate him. I was selected the following year, and it was the greatest day of my father's life – to know that his son had been picked to play for Scotland. My brother Bob played for the Scottish League, which was a fine achievement, but my father was proud and emotional when he heard I was going to play for my country.

I was pleased for myself, naturally, because this was another important stage of my career and I knew that the higher I could raise myself as a player the better would be my chances of becoming a manager later on. I was always thinking ahead. But when I was chosen to play for Scotland I was more pleased for my family, my mother and father, brothers and sisters, aunties and uncles. I knew how pleased they would be and it made them feel proud when I brought home my international cap and international jersey.

My first appearance for Scotland was the one at Wembley two weeks before the 1938 Cup Final. I remember it vividly. Someone wrote in a newspaper that it was the best England team they could possibly have picked, so that was something to start with – and we beat them.

I was a hard player, but I played the ball, and if you play the ball you'll win the ball and you'll have the man too. But if you play the man, that's wrong. Wilf Copping played for England that day, and he was a well-known hard man. The grass was short, the ground was quick, and I was playing the ball. The next thing I knew, Copping had done me down the front of my right leg. He had burst my stocking – the shin-pad was out – and cut my leg. That was after about ten minutes, and it was my first impression of Copping. He was at left half and we came into contact in the middle of the field. I think the pitch was more responsible for what happened than anything, but I was surprised that he would do what he did to me in an international match. He was older than me and had a reputation. He didn't need to be playing at home to kick you – he would have kicked you in your own backyard or in your own chair. He had no fear at all. But while we were fighting for Scotland that day, we didn't go round trying to cripple people.

What Copping did stung me, but I didn't complain about him. I said to him, 'Oh, you're making the game a little more important.' Frank O'Donnell, who could look after himself, was annoyed at Copping and told him what he thought about it.

Copping had been after me and had caught me and I never contacted him again during the match. But he also hurt me when I played against him for Preston at Highbury on a Christmas Day. One of our players pulled out of a tackle for the ball and I had to go in to fight for it, and Copping caught me on my right ankle.

I was due to play another match the following day, but my ankle had blown up to an awful size. We went from London up to Fleetwood and Bill Scott said, 'We'll have a try-out in the morning.'

'What do you mean, a try-out?' I asked him, and I soon found out. Next morning my ankle was still badly swollen, and Bill got me a bigger boot to wear on my right foot. My normal size was six and a half, but I put on a size seven and a half or eight that day.

For years afterwards I played with my ankle bandaged and wore a gaiter over my right boot for extra support, and to this day my right ankle is bigger than my left because of what Copping did. My one regret is that he retired from the game before I had a chance to get my own back.

Tommy Walker got the goal against England, and I was close to him at the time. Frank O'Donnell nudged the ball down and Tommy hit it from about thirty yards out and it screeched into the roof of the net. There must have been fifty thousand or more Scottish people in the ground. With twenty minutes to go the roar started and it never stopped. I said to George Brown, 'George, we can't get beat now. How can you get beat for these people? We'll all play like two men now.'

The dressing-rooms were near Wembley Way then, and when we came out all the buses and cars were filled with Scottish supporters. It was tremendous, fantastic.

The next year I played against Ireland in Belfast, against Wales at Tynecastle, against Hungary at Ibrox, and finally against England at Hampden Park. We needed to win that game for the triple crown. We'd won in Ireland in a mud-heap and we'd beaten Wales in a mud-heap and we had caused some trouble with our strength.

But Jimmy Delaney called off playing at Hampden and that was a blow, because I felt that Delaney, Walker and myself together was a combination hard to deal with. Delaney was a clever winger, a player who went from Celtic to Manchester United late in his career and who won Cup medals in Scotland, England and Ireland. Walker was the great inside forward who played for Hearts and Chelsea. He was fast, courageous, good in the air and could belt the ball with both feet.

It poured with rain. The supporters brought newspapers with them as umbrellas, but they were still soaked to the skin. With perhaps less than twenty minutes to go we were winning 1–0, but Pat Beasley came and battered one for England. Matthews was very fit and was probing. He had already beaten a couple of fellows when I was making my way over from my position to the other side to delay him if he held on to the ball.

I got halfway between the goalpost and Matthews and he lobbed the ball over my head. Tommy Lawton was at the near post and smashed the ball and said, 'Get in, you so-and-so.' I could hear the rain swishing off the net, and if the ground had opened up and buried me I'd have been happy.

That moment was like doomsday. It was like a big bag of cement falling into the stomach. That was Lawton, of course, a great centre forward. And Matthews. So we weren't beaten by nobodies, we were beaten by players.

4 Acting Corporal

The war started on 3 September 1939, the day after my twenty-sixth birthday. I had played for Preston at Grimsby and on our way back on the bus on the Saturday night we stopped at Burnley for a meal. Even then there were hopes of peace. The old chairman, Mr Taylor, was optimistic about it.

Next morning I went to the ground for the usual Sunday-morning pine bath and massage (some people were trying to sweat the beer out of themselves while I was getting ready for the next game), and at eleven o'clock on the radio the Prime Minister said, 'We are now at war with Germany.' That afternoon Deepdale Road was filled with wagons from Preston barracks taking troops on their way to trains.

Having been a miner, I could have gone back to the pits. But I didn't know what to do. However, I got a job as a riveter with English Electric, who were making Hampden bombers. But I felt shut in and, though it was a reserved occupation, I said, 'I'm going,' and joined the RAF.

I was first stationed at Padgate, where I met up with Ellis Robinson, the great Yorkshire cricketer, and Willie McFadyen, who used to play for Motherwell and was forty when he played for Huddersfield against Preston in the FA Cup Final.

My aim in the services was to do my bit, whatever I could, and look after myself, to keep myself fit. I wasn't after promotion and all that stuff and I didn't take any advantages. I wasn't out late at night or missing for a day. I had discipline. I did the jobs I was asked to do. If I was asked to scrub floors or clean latrines, I did that better than the next chap. Some of the fellows were loitering about in the NAFFI, drinking beer, smoking cigarettes, eating rockcakes, while I was running about the lanes, keeping myself fit.

Then I went to St Athan, Barry Island, South Wales, and found a place near the docks where you could get steak, egg and chips, nourishing food. It was hard to get, but as long as I wasn't taking it off someone else's plate, that was all right. I was so intent on being fit that I was in as good condition then as I was before the war. During my time at St Athan I played for Scotland against England at Wembley. We drew, no score, and a newspaper made me the man of the match.

From St Athan I moved up to Manchester, which was the best camp I was in because it was full of sportsmen and the people were wonderful. I played football for the station team and we won the Manchester and District Services League. I also boxed for the camp. I was eleven stone five pounds, middleweight. I weigh only six pounds more nowadays. We won the Duke of Portland Cup for the camp. I was always interested in boxing – we had Benny Lynch in Scotland of course – and I used to pay a pound a year subscription to get *The Ring* magazine sent to me from America before the war. I gave my boxing trophy, a little cup, to Mr Taylor, the Preston chairman.

Manchester was a tremendous place and again I was able to get decent food. I had a pal down Cheetham Hill Road who got me steak and chips.

I went to an officer one day and said, 'Can I get leave this weekend? I'd like to go on Friday morning.'

He said, 'What are you doing?'

'Well, I'm playing for Scotland against England,' I said.

He gave me a suspicious look and said, 'You're a joker all right.'

So he didn't believe me and I had to bring out my letter from the Scottish FA which confirmed it. But he had his little fling before that, saying to people around him, 'I have got one in here, old boy.'

So I said, 'And I have got one here, too, old boy – it's a letter.'

About one or two o'clock one afternoon a green plane came over the top of the camp and stuck some bombs into it and machine-gunned the area too. They killed one or two and maimed a few, and if it had not been at lunchtime they would have killed hundreds in the hangar. That was the nearest we got to the battlefields.

I cried when I left Manchester. That was an unusual thing for me to do because I am not the crying type, but I had enjoyed myself so much and met so many wonderful, friendly people that it upset me to leave. My next stop was Arbroath, of all places, in the north of Scotland.

Boy, was it cold! I was there for about six weeks on a junior NCO's course and I played for East Fife during that time. Harry Johnston, from Blackpool, was at Arbroath for a short spell. He stayed in an old mill. You could get haddock and chips from the shops up there and I ate almost enough to last me for the rest of the war. But the NCO course was hard work, marching and bayonet fighting and everything.

The highest rank I reached was acting corporal – not very high, but I hadn't any ambition to reach any great rank. Even so, I was possibly a better example to the men than some of the sergeants were. I gave more advice than the sergeants did, and without the bull. I felt some of the boys were put upon. Some deserved it for being lazy and dirty, but some seemed to be victimized for the sake of it. I once stopped a man of equal rank to mine from victimizing a boy because of his faith. That was at Great Yarmouth, a recruiting depot. I stopped that man from being stupid.

After I left Arbroath I was on the staff at Great Yarmouth and a fellow called Sergeant Riley from the south of England was in charge of our recruiting wing. He was a round-faced fellow, a real character – I'll never forget him. Some of the recruits would come in without their uniforms and Sergeant Riley would look at them and say, 'What have I done to suffer this? Look at this lot. It's always me that gets them. They've got two left feet some of them.'

It was true that some of the boys could not co-ordinate their limbs. No disrespect to them, because they were intelligent fellows, but there are some things certain people can't do. I had an 'Awkward Squad', and the boys swung both arms at the same time and couldn't march in step. It was unbelievable. I nearly fell down laughing. I couldn't keep it in. I was vibrating.

I played a game or two for Norwich City when I was at Yarmouth (you could play for anyone during the war : registration was no problem) and when the recruiting depot closed I moved to Henlow in Bedfordshire, where there were two camps and a technical training school. Some boys from the Navy came there. They stayed in huts, slept in hammocks and washed their own clothes. Jack Crayston who was an officer, and his Arsenal team-mate, Laurie Scott, were in the other camp.

We had a camp football competition, which the Navy won. I refereed the final and I remember that big Ted Buckle, who went to Manchester United after the war, played in the match.

There was a fellow called Jack Mindel, whose father had been a professional boxer at one time, and Jack and I used a hut as a gymnasium. We sparred ten to twenty rounds a night and would then go out and get something to eat. We boxed hundreds of rounds, just to keep fit. Jack and I have been friends ever since.

I played some games for Luton when I was at Henlow, and Luton were very good to me. In fact I could have gone to Luton after the war as a player and later they wanted me to go there as manager. I also played for Arsenal during my stay at Henlow – I was in every game for them except one leg of the semi-final when they reached one of the war Cup Finals. All their own registered players were available for that Final, so I was left out. I was given a packet with money and tickets in it but I gave it back to them and said, 'You keep that. I wasn't playing for that. I played to keep my place in the team and now sentiment has come into it and you are playing your own players.' I didn't take the money or the tickets. I stood on the terraces and watched the game. Arsenal beat Charlton 7–1.

Highbury was a first-aid post then, and Billy Milne, the trainer, was in charge of it. There were beds and everything, so when I played at Arsenal I slept there on the Saturday night and had my breakfast, my bath, and then went back to the camp.

When I was about to be transferred from Henlow to Glasgow, I telephoned George Graham, who became Sir George Graham, secretary of the Scottish FA, from London, and told him I was coming back up to Scotland. Rangers played a game on the Monday afternoon and if I had known about it I would have caught an earlier train. As it was, I got to Glasgow on the Monday night.

As I walked along Central Station with my kit-bag a fellow said, 'You haven't seen Bill Shankly, have you?'

'News carries fast. I'm Bill Shankly,' I replied.

He said, 'Oh, Mr Turner of Partick Thistle would like to see you.' That was old Donald Turner, the secretary-manager.

'That was quick. How did you get to know?' I asked.

'George Graham told us,' he replied.

So within ten minutes of getting off the train, I was in the Locarno restaurant eating steak and chips with Partick Thistle directors and they told me about all the great young players they had for me to play with. 'I'll need to think it over,' I said.

Then they came out with the best one of all. They said, 'When you are in the services and you want to play football, you have to play with the team nearest to the camp.'

Well, this station was nearest to Partick Thistle's ground, but, if you had a tape-measure, you would find there was not much difference between Thistle's ground and one or two more. They had the route down as through Springburn, up Bilsland Drive on to Maryhill Road, and they had it all measured out, and the Scottish FA said, 'Yes, you have to play for the team nearest to the camp.'

So I signed for Partick Thistle and I was very glad I did. I enjoyed it. They did have some good young players and they arranged for me to have a cartilage out and paid for the operation themselves. That was a wonderful thing for them to do, because that left knee of mine was injured when I was playing for Preston at Halifax in a war Cup game. It was the only injury in my life that stopped me from playing.

c

I'll never forget the night after I had done it. I came from
Halifax to Manchester on a bus over the moors and my leg was
a terrible size. I went to Crumpsall Hospital and when they saw
the X-ray plates they thought at first I had a broken knee-cap.
They put a plaster on it, of course, and when the fluid drained
away and the swelling went down, the plaster was wobbling up
and down.

The sister was Irish, and I stood on one leg saying, 'How can
my leg be broken?'

She said, 'You get back into bed.' I gave her a dog's life and I
was out inside a week.

When I got back to the camp in Manchester, the old MO
said, 'I don't think you will play again.' He thought that was
the end of Bill Shankly's football career. But Thistle arranged
for the cartilage to be taken out at a nursing home in Glasgow.
I recovered and, to recompense Thistle, I helped them to win
the Summer Cup. We beat Hibernian 2–0 at Hampden in the
final.

During my time in the RAF one of the most important events
in my life happened. I met my wife, Agnes, or 'Ness' as I call
her. Ness was in the WRAF and we were stationed at the same
camp. We met when I was working hard to get fit again after the
operation. Jock Porter, the Scottish heavyweight champion, was
at the camp and we used to do a lot of jogging together. Jock
used to carry weights in his hands to help strengthen his arms
and we ran around the lanes up near Kirkintilloch.

One day Ness saw us running in our track suits and said to
a corporal called Hughie Hamilton, 'Who are those fellows?
I see them every day going out of the gates.'

He said, 'That's Bill Shankly.'

'Aye?' said Ness.

'You know him, he's an international footballer,' said Corporal
Hamilton.

But Ness had never heard of me. She didn't know anything
about football and to her, Jock and I looked like a couple of nut-
cases. 'They must be off their heads,' she said.

I pestered her from then on. I used to take over toasted cheese to her section. We were married in Glasgow, Nessie's home, in 1944. We had a week's leave but didn't go away on honeymoon – it was the week before the football season!

Jock Porter said to me one day, 'I'm going to fight Bruce Woodcock.'

'Keep away from Bruce Woodcock, for Christ's sake,' I told him.

'I gave Bruce some advice, you know,' said Jock.

'Well, I'm giving you some – keep away from him!' I said.

Bruce Woodcock nearly killed Jock. He lasted three rounds and didn't come back for a week after that.

It was a good thing that Ness was not interested in football, though she went to a couple of games in Scotland before and after we were married. At Ibrox Park one day Thistle played well and we were winning 3–0, but the decisions went against us in the second half and Rangers got a 3–3 draw. There was a bit of a fracas and I'd 'done' Scot Symon. Scot played left half for Rangers and was a hard-tackling player – like Wilf Copping. In this game he was a bit rough on one of the young Thistle players, so I decided to play Scot hard. I had a few tackles on him, we spoke a few taut words and the crowd became agitated and was shouting and bawling.

After the match, Ness and I got in a taxi with a fellow called Joe, who was Rangers-mad and was angry because we had got a draw, which was like a win for Thistle and should have been a win really.

'Ah,' said Joe, 'Scot Symon – !'

Before he could say more I said, 'Listen, if Scot Symon was the champion of the world I might be the next champion.' That made Joe worse, of course, because of his allegiance to Rangers.

Nessie went to Celtic Park one day and left before the end because I was having a bit of a rough-house on the floor.

Another time, Thistle played Celtic at Firhill and somebody threw a beer-bottle over on to the greyhound track. I picked up the bottle and was kidding that I was going to throw it back. A policeman said, 'For Christ's sake, don't do that. You'll cause

a riot.' I turned towards the crowd and said, 'I know you lot.'
They were good-humoured.

On the Monday morning one of the boys at the camp, Johnny
Mulholland said, 'We know who threw that bottle. We caught
him. He's in for it now. We're going to punish him.'

I said, 'That's good, Johnny.'

He said, 'For missing you!'

The war ended when I was in Glasgow and I was demobbed
in January 1946 at Kirkham, near Preston. Our elder daughter,
Barbara, was born in Glasgow, in the same house as Ness, the
same bedroom, the same bed. She learned to walk at Preston.

I was demobbed on the Friday, stayed at my old digs in Preston,
and played against Everton on the Saturday in the FA Cup,
the season Derby County won it. It was a two-legged tie against
Everton. We beat them 2–1, then they beat us 1–0 at Goodison
Park the following Wednesday. So we played extra time. It was
still a draw, so we played to a finish – next goal the winner.

It was a penalty kick at the Gwladys Street end and the rain
was sheeting down and the pitch was skiddy. George Burnett
was in goal for Everton and I was taking the kick. I had the wind
and rain at my back and there was a bit of a slope at that end
of the ground. I thought, 'This is it.' Some of their players were
trying to put me off, saying things like, 'He puts it in there,
George.'

I said, 'George, I'll tell you where he puts them – he puts them
in the back of the net. If I don't score with this, George, I'm packing the game up here and now.'

I hit the ball with the side of my foot and it was maybe three
feet inside the post. It skidded in like a bullet. Wet day, heavy
ball – everything was perfect. I could have said, 'Listen, George,
I'm going to put it on that side. I'll give you a chance. You dive.'
And he still wouldn't have had a chance.

Ness moved down to Preston and we had nothing. Everybody
was looking after themselves after the war and that was one of
the lessons I got in life. It underlined what I had known right
from the beginning – you have got to stand on your own feet,
because nobody is going to give you anything.

5 Bitter End, New Beginnings

At one time I thought Preston North End was the greatest place in the world. It would have broken my heart to have left. But in the end I went without shedding a tear, bitter because I never got what I was promised.

Early in 1949 I was captain of Preston but I hadn't been in the team and they were near the bottom of the First Division. They brought me back and there was a terrible struggle. Tommy Finney had a number of injuries that season and missed a lot of games, which would have been a big blow for anybody.

The manager's job at Carlisle was vacant and I got the chance of taking it. I was thirty-five years old and had qualified as a masseur. I had a knowledge of physiology and anatomy to go with my experience as a player. I went to see the Carlisle board and they offered me fourteen pounds a week, which was what I was getting at Preston. Top wages. I told Preston all about it and they weren't very pleased of course.

I was due to get a benefit match and Tommy Finney said, 'Don't go. Stay here and I'll get you a benefit match and you'll get a good gate.' And I said, 'Well, I could do with it, Tommy, because in actual fact I've got bugger all. I've got nothing.'

So Tommy begged me not to go, but I knew it was right. I've never been in doubt about anything I've done or anywhere I've gone. That's lucky, because if you're ever in doubt and it means moving your job and your home, stay put. But I had no doubts.

I wanted to go, and Preston tried to persuade me with all kinds of things.

'You've got a benefit match,' they said. I said surely I could go to Carlisle and still have a benefit match. That was a simple thing. So I went to Carlisle in the March and I got no benefit match. I'd played all those games and I'd never been injured except in a wartime match, and I went to Carlisle because it was an opportunity, at thirty-five years of age, to start early as a manager.

I felt the people who were running Preston at the time had cheated me out of my benefit match and that was the biggest let-down of my life in football. It didn't need that to happen at Preston for me to think along these lines, but if I promise you something you'll get it.

What happened was a pity, because up until that point I couldn't have been luckier than to have worked with people like Tommy Curry and Billy Hampson at Carlisle and Bill Scott, Jim Metcalfe and James Taylor at Preston. And everything I did on the field was for the team. For myself, yes, but for the team first. If you play for the team first and foremost, you will get the rewards later on.

All the time I was preparing myself for the day when I would become a football manager. I had absorbed all the coaching systems at Preston and I knew what the game was all about. I also knew I could be a leader. I had confidence in my ability. I had not been sleeping. I had been working for the future. As far as I was concerned, it was simply a question of an opportunity presenting itself.

There are players in the game now who have probably reached the stage where they are thinking the way I thought then. Players like Frank McLintock, the Queen's Park Rangers defender, for instance. I do not know what Frank plans to do about his future, but he is a good example of a player with tremendous experience who is nearing the time when he must decide whether he stays in the game or tries something else. He has a tremendous will to win and looks like management material. He speaks well and, though he is a likeable chap, he can be hard as well.

A lot of people have given the impression of having exactly what it takes to become a successful manager, but it is a complex job and not too many match up to it. A man might have the ability to coach and teach and set an example, but he might go to the wrong club and find he is unable to cope. He might go to a place where there are all sorts of battles to fight – not football battles, but political battles and intrigue. He might also find difficulty in having to deal with players not much younger than himself.

Some fellows might get a good managerial job right away, while others will be unlucky and struggle. Matt Busby, for instance, got the chance of going to Manchester United. The ground was a bomb-site after the war, but the potential was there. Matt made the most of his opportunity and the potential of the club and made United the greatest. Other managers, myself included, have had to take a longer route to the top, by managing smaller clubs first.

My career as a manager took me to Carlisle, Grimsby, Workington and Huddersfield, but during my time with those clubs I never felt that Matt Busby or Stan Cullis, at Wolves, were better managers than me. Not for one minute. I don't mean to brag or boast. Matt and Stan are brilliant men, but I knew I had a system of playing and a system of training and I was clever enough to go on with it. I also knew how to deal with people. I don't like to domineer over people. I like them to respect me. I could speak simple common sense about the game and I could spot a player.

I have always applied the same basic formula to judging a player. First and foremost he must have ability and courage. One without the other is no good. I also look for physical fitness and a player who will work, who is prepared to struggle against the odds. There have been players, like Ian St John and Ron Yeats, whom I bought for Liverpool, whom I have seen once and said, 'That's enough. They'll do!' But if you could be that sure about every player the game would be too easy. There have been other cases when I have watched players many times, at home and away, before I have been completely satisfied that they had all the necessary qualities.

While I was playing, I was learning. I took a course through an agency in order to become a masseur, and I remember getting a telephone call from Ness when Preston were playing at Highbury one day to tell me I had passed the examinations. I knew a bit about human beings and what made them tick, what an athlete could stand, and I had assimilated all the modern training techniques at Preston. And then this job came at Carlisle.

A football manager is only a glorified trainer. On the Continent they call them 'coaches', and that's the right name. If a man can't go out and train a team in every aspect, coach players and tell them how to play, and know about injuries and how long they might take to mend, he's not a manager at all. He might as well go home and change his title, because that is the whole essence of the game. The rest is a waste of time. All the talk and the stuff you get from books is rubbish. Only the actual things that happen matter.

I had that knowledge. I had been with people who knew how to train teams and I had my own conception of human beings and psychology. I was as fit as anybody in England and when I returned to Carlisle I did all the training, played in the practice matches, did scouting, cleaned the boots, brushed out the bloody dressing-room, everything. I even burned all the training kit. It was stinking, so I got a big furnace and burned the lot. The players got everything new and what we couldn't get we ordered.

The old stand, like a pigeon loft, had deteriorated and was falling to pieces and the terraces were derelict, a terrible sight. But the club had a little money, £16,000, from selling Ivor Broadis, and we invested it well. We bought Billy Hogan from Manchester City – he came up here and they thought he was Stan Matthews – and we got Ernie Whittle and converted Geoff Twentyman from reserve-team wing half into centre half and it suited him fine.

We worked hard and had new training kit. When we were passing through Doncaster on our way to play at Lincoln I saw a sports shop, stopped the coach, and went in and bought a new set of playing kit and the team played in it at Lincoln. My aim was to make the players feel good – by letting them wear the best kit, eat the best, and stay in hotels if we could. Incidentally, my Uncle Billy was still a Carlisle director.

Ness and I started from scratch again with nothing. At Preston we were buying a house, but the club bought it to relieve us of the financial burden and then rented it to us. At Carlisle we moved into a club house, which wasn't the greatest. But Ness hadn't been away from home very long and missed Glasgow and we could get there in two hours on the train from Carlisle.

They were hard but happy days. I used to bring the playing kit home and Ness would wash it. We got one of those Bendix washing-machines, which were new then, and it was some operation to get it fixed in the house. We needed new pipes and everything, and I think all the engineers in Carlisle had to come to the house. It was brilliant though – automatic.

Ness was expecting our other child, Jeannette, at the time, and went into the nursing home. We hadn't had the machine long and I decided to do the washing. I bunged everything into hot water – blankets, vests, everything. Of course when they came out my daughter Barbara's vests were so small you wouldn't have got them on a doll. Everything had shrunk, and all the blankets were half-size.

Carlisle was good experience. We played in front of sixteen, seventeen and eighteen thousand people. The biggest crowds Carlisle had were when they were in the Third Division (North) – bigger than they got when they were in the First Division later.

Right from the start as a manager I tried to show that the fans are the people who matter. You've got to know how to treat them. If you don't do that then you're only wasting your time. You've got to have them on your side. The team, the manager and the people are all that matter.

I used to go on the Tannoy at a quarter to three to speak to the people every other week before the game. Instead of putting something in the programme, I spoke to them, explaining if we'd changed the team, how it had played in the last game. Everything. The supporters loved it – they lapped it up.

There was a man who wrote in one of the local papers who heard that an Irish player at Doncaster had a bad ankle and wouldn't be playing against us at Carlisle at Easter. He thought the player was Peter Doherty and put this in his paper, but in fact the injured Irishman was Joe Dubois. Peter Doherty playing for Doncaster would fill the Carlisle ground, so you can imagine how I felt when I read the paper. I went on the microphone and slated the man from the newspaper, who was sitting in the stand. I said, 'What are you trying to do – sabotage the club? Check your facts!'

The reserve team used to get wonderful results, like going to Sunderland and winning 4–0, and could draw crowds of six and seven thousand at home – bigger gates than Carlisle get now in the Second Division.

I was putting my ideas into operation, and the main thing was the way I tried to deal with players. I was determined to be fair with them, instead of victimizing them, punishing them, fining them, castigating them or humiliating them at the wrong time or in front of the wrong people.

I would not have favourites. A player could be my biggest enemy, but if he could play I would say he was great. If he didn't like me, it didn't make any difference to my judgement. Throughout my time at Preston I saw favouritism. 'Jimmy is a nice little chap,' they said, so Jimmy would play, even though he wasn't as good a player as Peter. I saw that happening and I saw that it was wrong.

Then there was the training to be streamlined and improved upon. The initial training is designed to get your body fit for the functions that will make you play better. Even at Preston players would be lapping round the pitch right to the last day of the season, and when I arrived at Carlisle their players were doing the same. I cut out all the monotonous soul-destroying stuff.

We had the use of a rugby pitch, a big car park made of ashes and a little field which we loaned from a farmer. Once the players were fit, we concentrated on ball-work and team-work, rolling the ball about instead of thumping it up the pitch predictably so big opposing defenders could say, 'Oh, thanks very much.'

Freddie Ford, the trainer, told a story. When I was at Carlisle rationing was still on and there was a farmer who used to bring us a few dozen eggs and a big lump of butter at the weekend. Freddie's job was to count out the eggs and cut the butter into chunks. He even had a little pair of scales. Having a reserve team, we had more players than we had butter and eggs, and consequently only twelve or thirteen of them had a share. That was a clue as to whether or not a player was in the team. One night, when Freddie had all the eggs and butter wrapped up, Dennis Stokoe, a useful player, was making his way to the cubby-hole to get his ration. 'You'd better wait, Dennis,' said Freddie – so Dennis knew then that he was dropped.

Accommodation was a problem. The club bought a big house and converted it into flats for players. The flats were supposed to be self-contained, but they weren't really. If the club had been able to afford houses for the players they would have been all the better for it. But it couldn't, so three or four families lived in the house.

I went up there one day with Freddie Ford and one of the boys said, 'It wouldn't be so bad if it was all cleared out and done up and I brought my own furniture . . .'

'Is that right, son?' I said.

'Yes, I'd be happy to do that.'

I had a talk with Freddie and when we left we found a junk-man and arranged for him to cart away all the furniture and carpets from the boy's flat and he put his own stuff in it and felt a lot better. All these things are important when you are running a team.

There was not much left of the season when I arrived, but we ended up drawing with Hull City, who won promotion. Twenty-man was a riot that day. I stayed for another two full seasons and we finished up with 62 points – and were third in the table behind Rotherham, who had 71 points, and Mansfield, 64. All those points, but only Rotherham went up of course, because in those days one club was promoted from the Third Division (North) and one from the Third (South).

In 1952 the manager's job at Grimsby Town was vacant and I applied for and got it. I made the move because Carlisle did not have the money to make progress and because I thought there was more potential at Grimsby. They were a famous club but had just been relegated to Division Three (North) and I felt that some of their players were better than Third Division standard. There was much more chance of success at Grimsby than there had been at Carlisle.

I thought, 'There must be something there, it's well established,' and having been to Grimsby, I knew it was hard for other teams to win there because of the characteristics of the ground and the time it took to get there. By the time you got to Grimsby you were half-beaten anyway!

Unfortunately Grimsby let some good players go, players I would have kept if I had got there sooner. But I was able to buy players. I paid Leicester City £4000 for Jimmy Hernon, a skinny little boy who played inside left and who reminded me a little of the great Wilf Mannion. Jimmy was a brilliant player and he scored fourteen goals one season, most of them with his head. I picked up Willie Brown from Preston, and I knew I couldn't go wrong with Willie because we had played in the same team. Willie was a big, strong right back. I had seen Walter Galbraith playing left back for Queen's Park in Scotland and he had what I was looking for. He was quick and cunning and could tackle.

Though Grimsby had sold players, I still had some very good boys to work with. There was Stan Lloyd, who wore number seven on his back but played deep because he wasn't particularly fast. Stan was small and clever and could pick up the ball in deep positions and distribute it well. To more than compensate for Stan's lack of pace, we had Jimmy Bloomer, a tremendously fast inside right. Jimmy, a Scottish boy, had a great partnership with the centre forward, Billy Cairns, from Gateshead. At that time Billy was the best player in England in the air. He was equal to Dixie Dean at heading the ball and Jimmy played off Billy, taking advantage of the flicks from Billy's head. They were to Grimsby then what John Toshack and Kevin Keegan became to Liverpool later. At right half we had Reg Scotson, an enthusiastic player from Sunderland. Reg was five feet ten inches and put everything into his game. Duncan McMillan, from Celtic, a most reliable player, was at centre half. On the left side of the field we had a trio of players who combined to give nightmares to the opposition. There was Paddy Johnston, an Irish boy, at left half and, in front of Paddy, there was winger Jimmy Maddison from Darlington. When they got together with Jimmy Hernon, they caused havoc.

Stan Ashurst, the goalkeeper, broke a finger in the first match of a season, and I brought in George Tweedy when he was forty-two years old. George was one of the greatest ever goalkeepers. On his day he was in the class of Frank Swift. George stood over six feet and had hands like shovels. Nobody rushed to shoulder-charge George.

I will never forget the day we lost Ashurst with that broken finger. Lincoln City were the visitors and we ended up with nine men, having lost another player with a broken leg, and were beaten. The next week we went to Lincoln and beat them. But Lincoln won promotion with sixty-nine points. We had sixty-six points and were runners-up – all those points and nothing to show for them. That was shocking and it was also sad.

It was sad because that Grimsby team was, pound for pound and class for class, the best football team I have seen in England since the war. In the league they were in they played football nobody else could play. Everything was measured, planned and perfected, and you could not wish to see more entertaining football.

We had more experience than youth, a team of players who knew what they were doing, every trick, every movement. And we caused some trouble and gave some exhibitions. We beat Halifax 8–0 one day. Halifax, and other teams, chased after our players with their tongues hanging out, thinking, 'What the hell will they do next?' It was a strong league, with teams like Lincoln, Stockport, Doncaster and Rotherham.

One day the gates were closed with twenty-seven thousand

people in the ground when we played Stockport County at a time when both clubs were fighting for promotion. Andy Beattie, my friend from the days at Preston, was manager of Stockport then. We gave them a drubbing at Grimsby and drew at Stockport.

The Grimsby team was fit and happy and in training we played five-a-side games as if our lives were at stake. We used to play for an hour at a time. We worked on throw-ins and were more dangerous from the corner kicks against us than the ones for us. We had a ploy – and the men to use it.

Maddison, who was a great kicker of the ball, was kept just outside our penalty box, along with Bloomer, who could run, and Cairns, who was a brilliant header of the ball. Whoever won the ball – it could have been Hernon – the first ploy was to poke it to Maddison. That was Bloomer's sign. When we got possession of the ball from the corner, Bloomer started off trotting and running through the middle, over the halfway line. By the time the ball got to Maddison, Cairns had also got forward, and Maddison would pump the ball up high for Cairns to flick on with his head. By that time Bloomer was in his stride. He scored umpteen goals from corner kicks awarded against us.

We had players capable of trying things like that. It's pointless asking players to do things beyond their capabilities. You are only wasting your time.

After just over two seasons at Grimsby I could see that the players were getting on a bit and that the club might not have enough money to replace them satisfactorily. Then Workington threw out a challenge to me. They were struggling at the bottom of the Third Division (North) and were threatened with extinction. There was only one man they thought could save them, and that was me, so they offered me a bonus if I saved them.

I had done as much as I could do at Grimsby and, at this time, Ness and I were just a little bit homesick and the job at Workington would take us a bit nearer to Scotland again. I knew I was taking a bit of a risk with my career in going to a club at the bottom of the League, but it was a challenge and there was the bonus. The Workington job gave me good experience.

I remember the first night I went to the ground. I opened the door, put my hand up to the wall and was feeling around. A fellow said to me, 'What are you doing?'

'I'm putting on the light.'

'There's gas in here,' said the fellow.

Bloody gas! Next I heard a noise outside and said, 'What's going on?'

'That's the Rugby League,' he replied.

'What do you mean, it's the Rugby League?' I said. I nearly went mad. I didn't know about that. I went outside and saw Gus Risman.

'What the hell are you doing?' I said.

'We're scrumming.'

'Christ,' I said, 'there's a game on Saturday here. What are you going to do?'

So I had to sit down and try to get rid of them. They trained on the pitch on the Thursday night and made a hell of a mess of it. I nearly got one match put off, a cup-tie against St Helens, but I couldn't shift them, even though I tried, because they paid so much money a year to the club for the use of the ground.

I knew there was a player who could help me to save Workington, and I went to Lincoln City and paid them £3200 for Ernie Whittle, a crafty little player from Stanley in the north-east of England. Ernie was no more than five feet four inches tall, but he was a great kicker of a ball. He scored fourteen goals, enough to keep Workington in the League.

By the following Christmas, Workington were at the top of the division. So again I had a team that was working. Not half! They were terrific boys – fellows like Whittle, George Aitken, Rex Dunlop, Jimmy Dailey and Hughie Cameron. A bunch of experienced players similar to the ones at Grimsby. We didn't get promotion, but we won the local Derby at Carlisle 4–0. And we beat Port Vale, who were promoted, 2–0. We played well and I was elated.

A football manager's working day involves him in the lives of so many other people: players, directors and supporters. I always made an early start. At Workington I lived about a mile from the ground and I walked there in the morning, walked back home for lunch, walked back to work in the afternoon and walked back home at night.

My first job would be to scan through the mail to see if there was anything of vital importance to be dealt with quickly. Then I would move on to the most important part of the job, the training of the players and a check on the progress made by those being treated for injuries.

After training, there might be people to see, and I would deal with the mail. I used a typewriter to answer the letters, but if it was possible I would telephone people instead of writing to them. I always wrote in answer to letters from supporters or football followers in general, but when I was dealing with business people I preferred to speak to them rather than write to them. I was given a tip by someone a long time ago. I was advised to give as little as possible in writing, just as a precaution. I am not suggesting I don't trust people, but there are some who like to show letters around. But, whether I wrote to people or spoke to them on the phone, if I said I would do something I did it, and if I said I would not do something, I did not do it.

Workington was a shoestring club. The money-making sweeps, the daily draw and things like that, had been halted by the Government while they sorted them out and limited them to a certain amount. But we survived.

The secretary was part-time and there was no one at the ground to answer the telephone if I wasn't there. The secretary made out the wage-packets and I used to keep them in the office. He made them out and I drew the money from the bank. I used to walk down the main street with the money in a bag every Thursday and think, 'I'm bound to get attacked one day.' But then I'd think, 'No, if they took all the wages they'd be getting nothing.'

I would walk down the street past the unemployed men, who would be sitting around smoking cigarettes. Sometimes I almost had to lift them out of the way to get past them. I used to stand and have a chat with them, with the money in the bag. Then I'd go back to the ground and put the money in the packets – *x* pounds, a ten-bob note and a half-crown. I would carry the packets around in my pockets, because there was no safe, and pay the players.

The board was laced with Rugby League directors and there were meetings with thirteen or fourteen directors present. They were not like ordinary board meetings. There were always arguments and some queer things were said. They were funny, better than going to the pictures. The chairman, Ernie Smith, would have an argument and resign every week. I said to him, 'You keep resigning – but you keep coming back.'

Each day a manager is building towards the next match and at the same time carrying a broad picture of the club's affairs in his mind. The manager's report is the most important part of all board meetings, because the running of the team is what really counts. I always kept typed reports on players for reference, and at every board meeting I would discuss the previous match in detail and sum up the performance of each individual player. I would then tell the directors of any inquiries I might have had from other managers about our players and inform them of inquiries I had made myself with a view to signing players. I would then discuss with the directors the scouting reports.

It was not easy being the manager of a club like Workington. The nearest places you could go to see a game, apart from Carlisle, were Preston, down twisting, turning roads, or Newcastle, which was another long journey. To play at Lincoln we used to leave at seven o'clock in the morning and get back the same night.

But we made the best of it. Deep down, I enjoyed it.

6 Law and Wilson

Andy Beattie is a great friend of mine and one of the most honest fellows under the sun. He has principles and sticks to them. If Andy says something to you, then you can trust your life that it will happen. He never deceived or cheated anybody in his life. As time went by and I recalled certain things that had happened I had an even greater appreciation of the man.

When I was at Workington, Andy was having a bit of a struggle as manager of Huddersfield Town. He's an independent chap, so when he admitted he was struggling, then that was authentic.

One day, right out of the blue, Andy telephoned me and said, 'Would you come down and be assistant to me? Eddie Boot is here. I think we can manage it.'

I jumped at the chance, because I had known Andy for years, from the days when we both played for Preston and Scotland. Andy had arrived at Preston shortly after I joined the club. He came straight from a junior team in Aberdeen around 1934. We got to know each other fairly quickly. We were round about the same age, but I was already playing in Preston's first team and I used to try to keep an eye on Scottish boys who joined the club. There were two I remember who were there, Willie Hamilton and Johnny Boyle. I was single at that time, and I used to take the boys to Blackpool to see the shows and we'd visit each other's homes in Scotland sometimes during the summer.

It was not long before Andy was in the first team. He came to the club as a forward but was converted to full back, and he played behind me. He was selected for Scotland before me, but we shared a lot of moments on the field together. At Preston the players had a saying before the matches: 'Let's all be captains today.' That was our attitude. One player would carry the ball and call the toss of the coin, but the team was successful because we all played as if we were the captain.

Now Andy was at the bottom of the First Division and he wanted me to help him. He was offering me an opportunity. He was offering me a partnership and he said that if it ever came to the point where he found another club, he would put my name forward to take over from him.

I said, 'Yes, I'll do it Andy.'

When I arrived at Huddersfield I was put in charge of the reserve team, though I mixed in with the first team during the week as well to try to boost morale. The unfortunate thing, I feel, is that Andy and I didn't work together with the first team all the time.

Andy thought the team was going to stay in the First Division and he wanted me to prepare boys like Denis Law and Ramon Wilson, who were to become great players later on. So Andy and coach Eddie Boot continued to travel with the first team, while I put to work my systems of training with the reserves.

The idea was that when the team escaped the threat of relegation Andy and I would start building together. Andy is a quieter type than me, but we complement each other. Though he is not as boisterous as I am, Andy commands authority. Given time, we could have been one of the strongest partnerships in football, like Matt Busby and Jimmy Murphy at Manchester United. Andy would also have made certain that I was his equal financially. He was the type who would have been quite happy for his partner to have been as well-off as himself and to have shared fully in any success.

Putting me in charge of the reserve team at first possibly helped the club in the long term, but it was too late at the time. The damage had been done, and Huddersfield went down to the Second Division.

Huddersfield won their last match of the season at Tottenham with ten men, and if Preston had drawn at home against Aston Villa that day, Huddersfield would have stayed in the First Division. But Villa beat Preston – and Tommy Finney missed a penalty. So our fantastic result at Tottenham was eclipsed by a hell of a result at Preston.

The following season I was still looking after the reserves and had pushed one or two players through to the first team. The reserves were doing well. They had played sixteen matches and were undefeated.

One Saturday night after a reserve-team match I got a telephone call asking me to go back to the ground. The chairman, Bernard Newman, met me and said, 'Would you like to be manager? Andy's finished. We're offering the job to you.'

I accepted the job, assuming that Huddersfield had already made arrangements with Andy and that Andy knew I would be getting the job.

When I left the ground I went round to Andy's house and I thought we would discuss what had happened. When I first went to Huddersfield I used to stay at the house next-door to Andy's, so I was a frequent visitor.

I was surprised that Andy had packed in and was waiting for him to say something. We sat in the house together and talked about this and that, but the manager's job was never mentioned. I was waiting for Andy to say, 'Oh, you've done it. You've got the job. Good luck,' or something like that. Then I would have said, 'I'm sorry about this, Andy. I should have come to see you before I accepted it.'

Nothing was said. I knew I was the new manager, he knew I was the new manager, but we never mentioned it. It was a kind of mutual embarrassment. It could have been my fault or it could have been his fault.

How I got that job is one of my biggest regrets. In some way I felt as if I might have let Andy down. I was embarrassed by the way it was done. I'm not suggesting that it was done dirtily, or that it was the chairman's fault. I took it for granted that they had told Andy all about it and he was agreeable. But it would still have been better if it had been done when Andy was there with me to hear it, if we'd had a get-together before it came out into the open, or if they had said, 'Look, Andy is finishing and you are the manager.' That would have been better for me, but it wasn't done that way and Andy was the one fellow you would never let down, because he would never have done that to you.

The chairman wasn't embarrassed and nobody else was, so it looked as though Andy was quite satisfied with the situation. Maybe that's why he didn't bring it up. He had said that if he packed in, the job would be mine, and, since he was a man of his word, I assumed that's what had happened.

It was sad. Who knows, if the chairman, Andy and myself had been able to discuss the whole situation beforehand, things might have worked out differently. The partnership might still have gone on and we would have been capable of pitting our wits against any team.

Andy and I remained close friends and later in the book you will read how he scouted for me and came up with a player who was a real bonus. But we have never discussed that Saturday night in Huddersfield, when he left and I took his job.

My first game as manager of Huddersfield was at Barnsley and I think we beat them 5-0. I remember the papers saying 'miracle-worker' and that kind of stuff. That was just the beginning, and we didn't need very much to make us a team because we had an array of talent on our books.

Bill McGarry was the first-team captain, and we had Law, Wilson, Mick O'Grady, Clive Clark, Les Massie, Kevin McHale and Kenny Taylor. Young Wilson had number six on his back and I put him back to number three in the reserves. And I brought Law into the reserve team at fifteen and played him with number eleven on his back so that I wouldn't take too much out of him.

Law and McHale were both sixteen years old when I brought them into the first team. They formed the right wing partnership when we played at Notts County. It was around Christmas time and I walked from the hotel in Nottingham Town to the ground with the two boys. It wasn't far. We won the game and they both played well.

I never saw Denis wearing glasses, except in a photograph of him sitting on the reserves bench during a Scottish schoolboy international match, but the story of his arrival at Huddersfield is famous of course.

Andy Beattie's brother, Lawrence, was scouting for the club in Aberdeen and had seen Denis playing in juvenile football up there. This was before I arrived, but when Lawrence came down to Huddersfield with Denis, Eddie Brennan, who worked in the office, was sent to the station to meet them and brought them to the ground. Eddie went into the office apparently, and said to Andy, 'I think your brother has made a mistake and brought the wrong man. You are going to faint when you see him.'

Denis was six and a half stone, skinny, and had on little iron-rimmed glasses and had a squint. But when Andy saw him running about playing the next day, he was like a weasel. He was in and out. He looked as though he was going through all their legs.

When I came Denis was in the junior team. They played Manchester United in the Youth Cup once under lights at Huddersfield, and Law and McHale gave United a terrible night I believe, even though United won. Matt Busby was very impressed and was trying to buy Law then. I brought Denis into the reserve team and one day at West Bromwich Tommy Glidden, who played for West Brom. in an FA Cup Final and later became a director, was sitting next to me. Law was giving the full back a dog's life and Tommy said, 'Who is this?'

'Oh, he is only fifteen,' I replied.

Tommy said, 'Oh, you're joking. Look I'll give you money for him now.'

'No, Tommy,' I said, 'you'll never buy him. Nobody will buy him. If Huddersfield Town are going to get anywhere, they need him, and more.'

Right from the start Denis stood out with his enthusiasm and will to win – nastiness, if you like. He would have died to have won. He would have kicked you to have won. He had a temper, and he was a terror – a bloody terror, with ability.

One Sunday I got a phone call from his landlady, a big woman who used to light a cigarette and never take it out of her mouth. 'You had better come down,' she said. 'Denis has just hit Billy McDonald.' So I got into my car and went down to his digs, which weren't too far away. Billy had a black eye of course. Big Gordon Lowe was in the same digs and I asked, 'What happened?' Gordon said Billy had said something about Denis and Denis had said that if Billy said the same again, it would happen again.

I said, 'Well, let that be a lesson to you, Billy – keep your mouth shut!'

That was it. Denis was going to do the same again. That was the kind of fellow he was.

The boys were playing table-tennis one afternoon and Eddie Boot and I were going through to the boot room. Denis challenged us to a game of football and I said, 'No, you have had enough training for the day.' But he insisted and in the end we went to the car park outside the ground and played a six-a-side game. Denis worked the usual stuff. He was in and out and we couldn't get near him.

That night there was a board meeting and Denis came to the ground. He walked down the road backwards. He couldn't walk properly because one of his calves had blown up like a balloon. We put him into hospital and it was a mysterious affair. The leg was out of shape. I think he had been doing too much training and playing for his size. When he recovered from that he was plagued by injuries in the front of his thighs, and we gave him injections to cure them.

Fellows like Stan Cullis, at Wolves, who fancied him strongly, were a bit dubious about his being able to stand up to the strain. There was nothing of him. But eventually he overcame all the set-backs, played for the first team at sixteen, and became the youngest ever Scottish international at eighteen.

The biggest problem we had was in signing Denis as a professional when he was seventeen. It was the end of the season

and Denis, still an amateur, was free. There was no protection
for the club and the whole thing was buzzing. Other clubs would
go to see his father and mother. People would drive up to Aberdeen to offer them all kinds of things. He didn't need to sign for
us. He could have walked away. I had been reasonably good to
him. I had helped him. I had got suitable digs for him, advised
him what to eat and talked to him about the game. I think he will
admit to that.

We were due to play in an FA cup-tie, and the whole thing
started – 'Who is he going to sign for?' Rangers, Celtic, all the
top teams of that time were mentioned. I got in touch with the
Football League and the Football Association and, whilst they
couldn't do very much about it, they said, 'Well Huddersfield
Town had him, brought him along, and if there is any under-
hand stuff, we will be on the side of Huddersfield Town. If we
get a registration from anybody else, we'll do what we can to be
fair.'

It was obviously going to be a difficult job to keep him. His
father and brother-in-law came down to see the cup-tie, which
was against Peterborough, who were then non-League. I went to
meet the pair of them at Leeds Station on the Friday and all the
newspaper men were there, photographers, and reporters pushing
and asking, 'Who is he going to sign for?' There was one who
started on about it in the toilet and I pushed him into the urinal.
His bottom was wet, I can tell you.

We took Denis's father and brother-in-law over to the chairman's cloth factory near to the ground. Mr Newman gave them
some suit lengths and some drinks. Denis's father had a few
whiskies and then we drove to the ground and talked before
taking them to the George Hotel. Next day we won the match
and Denis played well, and I saw the Law family at the George
Hotel on the Sunday. I arrived in the morning and we talked
things over until about nine at night, when Denis's father and
brother-in-law were due to leave to catch the train back to
Aberdeen.

I told them that I had been in touch with the football authorities and that they would be watching events. I talked about how

Huddersfield had done all they could for Denis and that they were not the wealthiest club in the world, so if he went some-where else it would not look too good. I told Denis not to start off on the wrong foot. 'I didn't make you, son, and Andy Beattie didn't make you. But I will tell you something – we helped,' I said.

He signed the forms that night, and they were completed the next day. But the big clubs were always after him and the offers kept rolling in.

Ramon Wilson had not long been demobbed from the Army when I went to Huddersfield. He was twenty, and I converted him from wing half to left full back in the reserve team and of course he turned out to be one of the greatest full backs of all time. He lived near me, in fact I went down to Ramon's house to tell him when he got his first cap for England.

Wilson was in the first team before Denis, but their careers soon began to run parallel. When they played against each other in a five-a-side game, what a battle of wits it was! And it was debatable who was the better. It was worth a pound to watch them in those games.

Before Denis came into prominence, Ramon was in our team at Sheffield Wednesday, where Harry Catterick was then manager. Both teams were running for promotion. At half-time a well-known scout from Chelsea called Jimmy Thompson – he picked up a lot of players, including Jimmy Greaves – came up to me near the stairs at Hillsborough. I remember he was wearing brown boots with a black suit.

'Oh,' said Jimmy, 'what about this fellow Wilson?'

'We don't usually transfer them at half-time,' I said and left him.

So Monday morning came and I went to the ground. Jimmy Thompson had got there before me. I opened the door and he hung up his coat before I could hang up mine. 'Wait a minute,' I said. 'Take it easy.'

Jimmy, a real Cockney character, a likeable fellow and a very good judge of a player, hung around Huddersfield for days, watching us train. He was after Wilson, but I remember him peering through the mist one morning and saying, 'Oh, that's Law; that's Law.'

'I can get you run out of the game for this, you know,' I said. 'You're poaching. You're not going to catch anything. The game-keeper will catch you, that's what will happen to you with your bloody poaching.'

In Jimmy's case I was only saying that as a joke, because he was around the ground so often. But there has always been poach-ing of players and I'm sure there always will be. It used to happen a lot with schoolboy international players, for instance. There was always a big rush to sign these boys, but only a few used to get them. Certain people got them and I don't know how they managed it. I have also heard the word 'tapping', which is used to allege that clubs have got word to players that they want to sign them. Perhaps it would be best for me to say that there are ways and means of getting players, and certain people would use these ways and means.

Jimmy Thompson's persistence continued. Huddersfield were due to have a board meeting one day, and he said, 'Ted is com-ing up.'

'Oh yes?' I said. 'Well he is wasting his time.'

Chelsea were struggling and Ted Drake did come up, saw the board at five o'clock and got no joy.

Harry Catterick also fancied Wilson. One night I went to see Wolves play Sheffield Wednesday reserves. I think Stan Cullis was trying to do deals as well. Law was being reviewed. 'I'm look-ing at your reserve team, Stan, to see what you have got,' I told him. Don Megson played for Sheffield Wednesday reserves that night and what a game he had. What a strong, rugged fellow. He was about the same age as Ramon, but bigger.

Harry had offered us a good sum for Wilson and I was think-ing, 'That money and this fellow Megson – what a bet!' We needed the money and Megson would have done a job for us. But the following week Megson was in Wednesday's first team – and was never out after that.

Many times I could have sold Wilson and Law, but I didn't. Johnny Carey, then manager of Everton, offered £45,000 for

Law, which was good money for a boy of seventeen. We had a board meeting and one of the directors said, 'That is a lot of brass.'

'Listen,' I said. 'Get out your diary and put this down. If you think that is a lot of brass for Law, you have a commodity and you don't know its value, which is a bad job. Put in your diary that one day Law will be transferred for £100,000.'

That was in 1956, and when I left Huddersfield, Denis was transferred to Manchester City for £55,000, from City to Turin for £100,000, and from Turin to Manchester United for £116,000. If it had been the same Law now, the fee would have been £500,000. Wilson was eventually transferred to Everton for around £40,000 in 1964.

One day I will never forget is 6 February 1958, the day of the Munich air disaster. I was at Huddersfield's ground at half past four that afternoon, and I had a telephone call from one of the pressmen. He told me Manchester United's plane had crashed and possibly all were lost.

Right away I went home and sat in front of the television, waiting for more news. I heard Mr Harold Hardman, who was then the United chairman, say that Matt Busby had died. I was shaken. That came as a terrible shock. I couldn't believe it. Then, when the situation became a bit clearer, the news was that several players and officials had died but that Matt was still fighting for his life.

The tragedy of Munich stunned everyone. Twenty-three people died from their injuries, including eight United players. Matt survived. Not only did he survive, but he built a new team, his third great team. A strong man, mentally and physically, but it is hard to imagine what he must have gone through in that hospital in Munich, not only from the pain of his own terrible injuries, but also from the knowledge that so many of his wonderful players had gone.

I had played alongside Matt when he was a wing half in the Scotland team and I had played against Matt's United team after the war – the team that included players like Johnny Morris, Jack Rowley and Stan Pearson. After the war, when

other teams were trying to get rid of their old players – teams like
Preston, for instance – Manchester United kept theirs. Matt even
went out and bought one, Jimmy Delaney.

Then he started to build, turning his attention to schoolboys,
and producing the brilliant Babes who crashed at Munich.
Tommy Curry, the United trainer and the man who did so much
for me when I was a player at Carlisle, lost his life in the crash.
Whenever Preston played United after the war, I used to take
Tommy a couple of dozen eggs. They were scarce in those days,
but I knew one or two people around Preston who could get
them for me, and I took them to Tommy because he had been
so good to me when I was a boy.

Matt was a crusader for European football, and of course the
United team was on its way from a match in Belgrade when the
tragedy happened. United did a great job for football in England.
They were the visionaries. I remember Mr Hardman going to
football meetings in London and asking for more money to be
allowed to be paid as incentives for players in European com-
petitions. People were so narrow-minded then that it was hard
for United to break down the apathy towards European football.
But United were right. Matt's vision became reality.

At this time I was still waiting for my opportunity in the big
time, but one of the most amazing games I have ever seen was
at Charlton when I was the manager of Huddersfield. The kick-
off was at two o'clock and Charlton lost their centre half with
a dislocated shoulder. We were winning 5–1 with twenty-five
minutes to go, and the last part of the game was played in semi-
darkness. Wilson, McGarry and Kenny Taylor started to go upfield looking for more goals – and in no time we were losing 6–5.
We made it 6–6 and I thought, 'At least that's something,' but
they kicked off again, won a throw-in and boof! – they had
beaten us 7–6 with the last kick of the ball.

We beat Liverpool 5–0 with ten men one day. Taylor
damaged ligaments in the first five minutes, but that didn't stop
us. I remember the Liverpool directors leaving the ground in
single file, with their shoulders slumped, like a funeral procession.

But I said we couldn't have a team if we sold Law and Wilson and we needed very little extra to win the Second Division.

Eddie Boot and I drove up through the moors one night, up to Kendal and on to Falkirk to see Ron Yeats and Ian St John, who were playing against each other in a Scotland versus Scottish Second Division Select match. Ronnie was in the Second Division with Dundee United. I saw him before the game and I saw him on the field. The quickness – and the size of him! St John played for Scotland. He was a box of tricks, punchy and strong. What a battle they had!

I said to Eddie, 'Has it not been worthwhile to come up here and see this?'

'Oh, dear me, yes,' said Eddie.

Yeats and St John were the players Huddersfield needed, but they couldn't afford to buy them.

7 St John and Yeats

One day in 1959, when Huddersfield were playing Cardiff City, Tom (T. V.) Williams, who was then chairman of Liverpool, and Harry Latham, a director, came down the slope at Leeds Road to see me.

Mr Williams said, 'How would you like to manage the best club in the country?'

'Why, is Matt Busby packing up?' I asked.

At the time Liverpool were scratching around the top of the Second Division and there was obviously more potential and ambition there than there was at Huddersfield.

I knew the Liverpool people and I had seen some boxing contests at Anfield, Peter Kane fighting Jimmy Warnock and Ernie Roderick against the great Henry Armstrong. I had a nose operation in Liverpool before the war and the specialist had come over to Preston to finish the job. Liverpool was a city like the Scottish cities and the people were similar to the Scottish people. The football atmosphere was reminiscent of Celtic and Rangers.

Right away I knew that was it, though I told the Liverpool directors, 'I will consider it.' I had no doubts about going to Liverpool, no misgivings, and I did not have a contract at Huddersfield. But I did not rush into it.

Liverpool had a great crowd. I had been there and had heard them and I had thought, 'Oh, what a place!' But at that time, for a city the size of Liverpool and considering the potential support, the situation was appalling. The dyed-in-the-wool supporters were just hoping a miracle would happen and they would have something to cheer about. People were on the Kop shouting and bawling, but not with the same unity or humour or arrogance that made them famous later.

Everton were in the First Division, of course, and I went to Anfield to see a Liverpool Senior Cup game. Bobby Collins turned Liverpool inside out, Everton dusted them up, and the atmosphere was awful. The mockery was embarrassing. It was pathetic. But, deep down, here was something.

A month or two after I had seen T. V. Williams and Harry Latham it came to pass. I took the chance and went to Liverpool in the December. The ground was an eyesore. It needed renovating and cleaning up. I said to the groundsman, 'Where is your watering equipment?'

'There is none,' he said. 'We don't have equipment, because there is no water.'

There was a pipe from the visitors' dressing-room and a tap. But no facilities for watering the pitch. It cost about £3000 to put that right.

Tom Bush, the old Liverpool centre half, took Ness and me round to look at the houses and we called to see the training ground at Melwood. It was just a wilderness, but I said to Ness, 'Well, it's big and it can be developed. At least there is space here.'

The ground was not good enough for the public of Liverpool and the team was not good enough for the public of Liverpool. There was only potential. The people were thirsting for success. They had been in the doldrums too long. They had never won the FA Cup and they were in the Second Division.

My first job was to get the training staff together and talk to them. I had known Bob Paisley as a player. I knew Reuben Bennett through my brother Bob at Dundee and I knew Joe Fagan because I had played against him when he was with Manchester City and I had tried to sign him for Grimsby Town. I said, 'You must have been a good player, Joe, because I tried to sign you!' There was old Albert Shelley, who was looking after the dressing-rooms, and the secretary was Jimmy McInnes, who came from the same county as me and who had been succeeded in the Liverpool team by Bob Paisley.

'Now normally managers come into a club and bring their trainers with them,' I said. 'Well, I'm not going to do that. You fellows have been here, some of you a long time. I have my own training system and I will work in co-operation with you. I will lay down the plans and gradually we will all be on the same wavelength. I want one thing – I want loyalty. I don't want anybody to carry stories about anybody else. I'm sure I don't need to warn you about this, but if anyone tells me a story about someone else, the man with the story will get the sack. I don't care if he has been here for fifty years.

'I want everyone to be loyal to each other. Everything we do will be for Liverpool Football Club. That makes strength, and maybe one day we'll get the players we need as well.'

Ness and I didn't move into our house in Liverpool until the following February, and I still kept in touch with a Sunday-afternoon team I used to play for in Huddersfield. This was made up of men from outside professional football. It was their recreation. To play on Sunday was really and truly the highlight of their lives. We had trouble with the council, who were going to buy the park where we had our pitch, and I helped to organize a petition. But eventually the council had to build houses on the park. Houses were more important than our team.

Gradually I was getting to know Liverpool better, though right from the beginning I knew you could never kid the people. I used to go to Huddersfield every weekend until we got the house in Liverpool. One day, when I had only had the job about a month, I was driving around the streets in Liverpool. Eventually I stopped the car, opened the door and said to a little boy, 'Look, son, can you tell me where Anfield is, the Liverpool football ground?'

'Oh, it's Bill Shankly,' he said.

I couldn't believe that he had recognized me. I'd barely arrived.

1 Mother, father and the boys. (*From left*) John, Bill, Bob, Jimmy and Alec.

2 The Preston right half.

3 With Stanley Matthews.

4 Back row, sixth from left, the RAF middleweight.

5 FA Cup, Charity Shield, League Championship and Liverpool of the sixties. Back row (*from left*): Reuben Bennett (trainer), Geoff Strong, Gordon Milne, Chris Lawler, Tommy Lawrence, Gerry Byrne, Willie Stevenson, Joe Fagan (trainer). Front row: Bill Shankly, Ian Callaghan, Roger Hunt, Ron Yeats, Ian St John, Tommy Smith, Bobby Graham, Bob Paisley (coach).

6 Ian St John scoring the extra-time goal against Leeds that brought the
FA Cup to Liverpool for the first time.

7 The second great squad of players. Back row (*from left*): Steve Heighway, Phil Boersma, Frank Lane, Ray Clemence, Jack Whitham. Middle row: Kevin Keegan, Phil Thompson, John Toshack, Peter Thompson, John McLaughlin, Peter Cormack. Front row: Ian Callaghan, Emlyn Hughes, Tommy Smith, the boss, Alec Lindsay, Chris Lawler, Brian Hall.

8 Tea and talk with Tommy Smith (*left*) and Joe Laidlaw, of Carlisle United, before an FA disciplinary hearing.

9 Double-barrelled . . . Roger Hunt and Ian St John.

10 Peter Thompson
gathering momentum.

11 The Keegan touch . . . against Leeds United.

12 Caught out: This is Your Life, with Eamonn Andrews.

13 With Jack Dempsey and Billy Bremner – 'some half back line!'

4 With the FA Cup, 1974.

15 With Nessie and the OBE

16 'Clean 'em good boys!' Wembley 1974.

17 I never walked alone.

When I went to Melwood to take my first training session it was in a terrible state. There was an old wooden pavilion and an air-raid shelter and there were trees, hills and hollows, and grass long enough for Jimmy Melia to hide in standing up. It was a sorry wilderness. One pitch looked as if a couple of bombs had been dropped on it. 'The Germans were over here, were they?' I asked.

As time wore on, the place was levelled and cultivated and a suitable pavilion was built with proper changing facilities and a sauna bath. But that first day it was a sight, I can tell you. The front pitch was bare except for the middle. I was told this was a cricket pitch. 'I'll cricket you!' I said, and it was made into our five-a-side pitch.

Bill Fryer, of the *Daily Express,* was the first newspaper-man I saw at Melwood. He watched my first training session as we prepared for a game against Cardiff City on the following Saturday. It was December, so the players were fit through playing and the grounds were heavy. We jogged around until our bodies were warm, nothing strenuous, and then I brought out a couple of bags of footballs. I remember Jimmy Melia giggling with glee at the sight of them. The rest of the session was nothing but ball work, chipping, shooting, controlling, heading and movement with the ball. I told Bill Fryer that this was where a great team would be built.

After training we had tactical talks galore over in the old board-room at Anfield. It was so dark I called it 'the Morgue' and I said to Jimmy Melia, 'Watch you don't trip over the coffins!' It was the most important week of my life. Cardiff, a good side, beat us 4–0, and a tremendous thing happened after the game. Jimmy Melia (Jimmy will be getting swollen-headed!) said, 'We were so anxious to please you that we tried too hard. Everybody had enjoyed the week so much, it was wonderful, with the change of routine. We were over-anxious.'

But after only one match I knew that the team as a whole was not good enough. I made up my mind that we needed strengthening through the middle – a goalkeeper and a centre half who between them could stop goals, and somebody up front to create goals and score them.

At the same time we were overburdened with players. The maximum pay then was twenty pounds and the staff was too big. Within a month I had put down twenty-four names of players I thought should go and they went inside a year. It was not that I had anything against those boys, but it had to be done – transferring them, letting them go free, helping them to get other clubs.

Knowing what needed to be done was one thing. Convincing the directors was another. It is difficult to believe how hard I had to fight to make certain people realize the potential of the club. People who had been there years longer than me didn't realize it. It riled me and made me sick sometimes. They had been so unsuccessful that they were pessimistic, frightened to do anything. They had got into the position where they were scared, like gamblers on a losing streak who were afraid to bet anymore. I had to fight to make people realize that it was possible to be successful, and many times during my career with Liverpool I felt like saying, 'That will do, I will get my jacket on and go.'

I used to fight and argue and fight and argue and fight and argue until I thought, 'Is it worthwhile, all this fighting and arguing?' It is bad enough fighting against the opposition to win points, but the internal fights to make people realize what we were working for took me close to leaving many times. I knew it was going to be a hard job and I would never run away from a hard job. That would have been stupid and cowardly.

At the other clubs where I was manager I knew their limitations. I knew when it was no good, when it was pointless. But not at Liverpool. I could see what was possible and yet I had to convince people that they should not do everything on the cheap. 'Don't buy that balloon, it might burst. Buy a better balloon.' 'Don't buy that ball, at five pounds, get the one at ten pounds, that's a better ball.' 'Don't go to cheap places, go to the best places. Only the best is good enough for Liverpool.'

The shareholders' meeting was a nightmare of criticism for the directors. The people were craving for success and I knew what was needed to get it. But I had problems trying to convince the directors that you couldn't get a good player for £3000.

I would tell them, 'Look, we need a goalkeeper.'

They would look doubtful and say, 'Oh, the one we have is good enough.'

That is how they went on every time I wanted to make a move in those early days. Some of the directors thought the club was all right. They were in the top half of the Second Division and were getting crowds of about twenty-four thousand.

Footballers' wages then were about twenty pounds a week and the club was solvent. But football was moving towards the new era when there would be no maximum on players' wages. The strong would become stronger and the weak would become weaker. I had to argue with the directors that we had to make progress. I had to convince them that if the players came on to the market they would have to give me the money to buy them.

The first player I tried to sign for Liverpool was Jack Charlton of Leeds United. I knew Jack very well and I had seen him play from his teens. We offered £18,000 for him, but Leeds wanted more. Not a lot more, but more than our people felt they could afford. If we had bought Jack we would have taken the backbone from Leeds and they would not have been the team they later became, because half their strength would have gone with Jack. No one could have visualized then that Leeds would become the force they did become, because in those days, before Don Revie lifted them, they were nothing at all. But if the Liverpool directors had managed to scrape together the extra money to buy Jack, Don's job would have been twice as difficult.

The manager is his own man. When he goes to a club he takes charge of the players and it is up to him to recommend the players to be bought and the players to be sold. He has got to prove his capabilities and convince the directors that what he says is right. Then the directors will respect him, because people respect strength. If a manager is weak and makes mistakes then he will lose his authority and will be kicked out. But even good managers have difficulties when they come up against businessmen with set ideas about how a club should be run.

No job is easy and I stuck it to the end, until the eventual triumphs, thanks mainly to a man of vision, a director who would only be associated with success and who was sick and tired of sitting in the pigsty we called a ground. That man was Eric Sawyer.

When Mr Sawyer, a big man in the Littlewoods organization, joined the board, he knew we were not good enough. We had lots of discussions together. Sometimes after a defeat we would go to the board-room and, over cups of coffee, we would talk over the affairs of the club, officially and unofficially. I told him of players who were available and others who might become available. I told him, 'These could be the foundations of the success we need.'

'Bill,' he said, 'if you can get the players, I'll get the money.'

Ron Yeats and Ian St John were still the players on my mind, but when we discussed possible transfer moves at board meetings the tune was still 'We can't afford them.'

That's when Mr Sawyer stepped in and said, 'We cannot afford *not* to buy them.'

At the end of my first full season at Liverpool, we finished third in the Second Division, and I was determined to sign players before the start of the following season.

One Sunday morning in 1961 the *Sunday Post* had the headline 'St John wants to go'. I was on the phone straight away and we were in Motherwell on the Monday night. Charlie Mitten came on the scene from Newcastle and tried to sign him, but we arranged the fee of £37,500 on the Monday night and signed St John the next day.

I said to Mr Sawyer, 'He's not just a good centre forward – he's the *only* centre forward in the game.'

A week after he signed, in May, St John played against Everton at Goodison Park in the Liverpool Senior Cup. Everton won 4–3 – but St John scored the three goals.

Yeats was in the Army and used to fly up from the south of England to play for Dundee United. Mr Sawyer and Sidney Reakes, another director, came with me to see about Yeats, and a Dundee director told me, 'No, we can't sell him.' But on the platform when we were returning to Liverpool another Dundee director, Duncan Hutchinson, whispered to me, 'I bet you could get him for £30,000.' A couple of days later, Dundee United phoned to say, 'You can have Yeats for £30,000.'

I phoned Mr Sawyer and he said, 'Right, do a deal.' I then phoned him back and said, 'We're meeting them in Edinburgh on Saturday.' He told me to tell Mr Williams and Mr Reakes to go with me. Reuben Bennett came too, and we travelled in Mr Reakes's car. At four o'clock on that Saturday night in July 1961 we signed him.

Big Ron was a fantastic-looking man, with black hair. The first time I saw him he was wearing a light-grey suit and I said, 'It should be Hollywood you're going to.' He looked as if he could outclass all the film stars. When he came to Liverpool, I got all the press boys and said, 'Go on, walk around him. He's a colossus!'

St John and Yeats were both twenty-three, and I said to Mr Sawyer, 'You sack me if they can't play. I'm telling you now, I'll stake my life on it.' And I told Mr Reakes, 'These players will not only win us promotion – they will win us the Cup as well.'

In 1960 we had paid £12,000 to Preston for Gordon Milne, a boy I had known from the cradle. I played alongside his father, Jimmy, who became Preston's manager, and we lived in the same street, Lowthorpe Road, near Preston's main stand. I can remember Gordon being born and growing up. I had been following his career and watching him and he had been putting in his foot and fighting for the ball. I saw him in a reserve match at Huddersfield one day, and he was a hardy little boy.

So we had Gordon, Jimmy Melia, Ronnie Moran, Johnny Morrissey, Alan A'Court, Gerry Byrne, Roger Hunt – the first time I ever saw him I said, 'Christ, this one can play!' – and though Bert Slater was in the first team, I had brought Tommy Lawrence from the background of the third team into goal for the reserves. We also had some other useful players on our books, but St John and Yeats were really the corner-stone, the beginning of the big march.

At the end of my first season, we finished third in the Second Division with fifty points. Next season, my first full one, we were

again third, with fifty-two points, and at the end of my third
season, 1961–62, we won the Second Division championship with
sixty-two points.

When we had won promotion to the First Division I went to a
shareholders' meeting and they were so thrilled about it that
they presented us with cigarette boxes. I told them, 'We got promotion, but you don't think that is satisfactory, do you? Next time we
come back here for presents we will have won the Big League,
the First Division.'

They looked at me the way the officer in the RAF had done when
I told him I wanted leave to play for Scotland against England,
as if to say, 'We've got a right one here.'

8 Body and Soul

It was hard to start with in the First Division, because we were not exactly prepared for it. We finished eighth in the first season, 1962–63. We started struggling and ran up against Leicester City, the best team in the Big League then. In fact I felt they were the only team we learned anything from.

Leicester were brilliant, playing cunning, crafty stuff, with players like Frank McLintock, Davie Gibson, Colin Appleton, Mike Stringfellow, Ian King, Steve Chalmers, Graham Cross, and Gordon Banks in goal of course. They played with intelligence and had players with the ability to make the most of plans. For instance, Cross and McLintock dovetailed perfectly, alternating between inside forward and right half, switching backwards and forwards.

Leicester didn't win the League championship, but they were the best team. Matt Gillies was the manager then and he did a great job. He deserved far more credit than he got. Matt has left football now and is a successful businessman.

We recovered towards the end of the season and jogged through the next – and in 1963–64 I made good my promise to the shareholders to return with the League championship.

At Easter I said, 'Right, boys, we've jogged along nicely. Let's go out and get it going. Never mind anything that happens – off you go!' We won seven games on the trot, running through teams and tearing them to pieces, and we rounded things off by drubbing Arsenal 5–0 at Anfield. The following season Liverpool brought home the FA Cup for the first time and the season after that the League championship was back at Anfield. All our hard work and close attention to detail was paying off.

I have many notebooks, accumulated over the years, which are filled with information. I picked up something from everybody in football I came into contact with, no matter who they were. If they said something or did something I thought was good, it would go down in the book. Whether or not they were conscious of what I was doing, I don't know. At home and abroad I would look and listen and think, 'That's not bad, but I'll add that to it and I will cut this out of it.'

This information has been invaluable in the training of our players and in our attitude towards winning matches. The philosophy and psychology was inbred, and I have always tried to make my thoughts about the game simple, sensible and clear. Paddy Crerand was once quoted in a newspaper as saying that when Jock Stein, Matt Busby and myself spoke about football, a six-year-old boy could understand us. We never tried to complicate people.

From the day I started at Anfield, the training was planned. We knew exactly what we were going to do each morning before we went to Melwood. Everything was tabulated on sheets of paper. This was the basis and everything stemmed from it. Bob Paisley, Joe Fagan, Reuben Bennett or myself would do something and one of the others would say, 'I think we could do without that,' or 'I think we could add this,' so the branches of our system sprouted out, just like a tree.

'Everything we do here is for a purpose,' I said, 'It has been tried and tested and it is so simple that anybody can understand it. But if you think it is so simple that it is not worth doing, then you are wrong. The simple things are the ones that count.'

As time went on I got through to everybody, the trainers and the players – I knew how to deal with them, when to speak to them and when to leave them alone. One day the trainers and myself were like psychiatrists. We analysed all the players – brainwashed them, if you like. We talked about their strengths and weaknesses, their good points and bad. It was like a confessional.

Reuben Bennett was the warm-up man and put the players through exercises for twenty minutes to half an hour at the start of training, before they did anything strenuous. That was common sense, of course, because you wouldn't rev up your car to the hilt when you first started driving it in the morning or you might blow a gasket. By the same rule, we didn't push players to the limit at first because they might have pulled muscles.

The initial training, which brings the strength for the start of a season, was the big test. That's the time when brains are needed most. If you do the wrong things then, the chances are you will have injuries. We had it down to a fine art, starting about five weeks and two days before the start of the season and building up gradually. All the players went by the standard of the slowest man, and nobody was allowed to sprint, dive or kick a ball until we felt they were ready.

I remember starting off the 1961–62 season shortly after I arrived. We won the first match against Bristol Rovers and Jimmy Melia said, 'That's the first time I've played the first match of a season and felt I could play another game right after it.' We then played Sunderland at Anfield and beat them 3–0. Brian Clough played for Sunderland and big Ronnie bottled him up. The following week we went to Sunderland and beat them 4–1. Then we hammered Newcastle twice.

The weather had been warm and it is easier to get fit in the hot weather. But the whole essence of our system was in feeling our way, testing to find out how long we should train and how much we should do before we started the really strenuous stuff.

I am what you might call an impatient patient man. I am impatient by nature, but I am not impatient when it comes to something important. I don't cut off my nose to spite my face. I don't do stupid things.

When the players were warmed up they were split into groups of six – A, B, C, D, E and F – and the trainers would supervise the group-training. At the beginning of each season the groups would be listed on the notice-board and the trainers would be given about a dozen foolscap pages of notes which they consulted each day.

Each group was put through a different function: A could be weight-training, B could be on skipping, C on jumping, D on squats, E on abdominal exercises and F on sprints. When the whistle was blown, the groups would move on to the next exercise until they had completed them all. They would then be put through a circuit of football functions: driving the ball, chipping it, controlling it, heading, and so on.

We then brought out training boards, which would be set up about fifteen yards apart and which would keep the ball in play and keep the players on the move all the time. If the ball beat the goalkeeper, it would hit a board and be back in play again. We also had a 'sweat box', using boards like the walls of a house, with players playing the ball off one wall and on to the next, similar movements to the ones I used to see Tommy Finney practise at the back of the stand at Preston. The ball was played against the boards, you controlled it, turned around, and took it again.

Before any particular exercise became a set part of our training, we would experiment. We used Roger Hunt as a guinea-pig with the boards. We placed them fifteen yards apart and told him to play the ball against one of the boards, take it, control it, turn, dribble up to the other board with just ten touches of the ball, play it against that board, pull it down, turn around, and dribble back again in ten touches and keep repeating the exercise.

We wanted to know how long this function should last. We were probing. After forty-five seconds, Roger, who was as strong as a bull, turned ashen and I said, 'That will do, son.' Later Roger could do that exercise for two minutes.

Then we tried three-a-side games with a pitch forty-five yards long and twenty-five yards wide. We played five minutes each way, and at first that was enough. But later the boys could play for half an hour and not be fatigued.

We proved that laborious sessions lasting for hours were nonsense. We devised a system where the players went through the functions in two-minute sessions over a period of fifteen to seventeen minutes. Two minutes, then half a minute's rest, and so on. After this we would round things off with five-a-side matches. 'Enjoy yourselves, boys,' I would say.

Each player was being watched. I would train in amongst them and I would know who wanted to train and who didn't. Ian Callaghan, for instance, had to be made to simmer down. He worked so hard on Saturdays that I had to say to him, 'Listen, son, you take it easy. Just you go through the motions.' Others had to be encouraged occasionally to do a little more. Once we were doing the functions with the boards and I noticed St John was just going through the motions, so I said to him, 'This is to speed you up, not slow you down!'

Tommy Lawrence was in goal by this time, of course, and while he was not a Ray Clemence, Tommy was full of craft and courage and did a wonderful job for us. He was invaluable. Sometimes I would advise Tommy that I thought he was getting a bit too heavy, but it was natural for him to carry weight. He trained hard, and we put the goalkeepers under pressure with four or five men battering balls at them. Instantaneous stuff, one shot after another. I'd shout, 'Come on, Tommy, get up on your bloody feet – I've given you half a second!'

He was down and up, down and up, diving continuously. Goalkeepers had more work in training than anybody else at Liverpool because they didn't do as much physical work on a Saturday. They could have eighty minutes when nothing was happening and be frozen near to death. I'd say to Tommy, 'Keep alive, son, keep warm. I'll give you some hot water-bottles to tie to your legs!'

Chris Lawler was a boy on the ground staff when I came to Liverpool and one day, when we were all ready to go down to Melwood on our bus, I saw Chris walking around Anfield. 'Where are you going?' I asked him.

'We work here,' he said, 'and train at night-time.'

'You work up here, cleaning the place up, and train at night-time? Well, you go now, son, and get all the ground-staff boys together and get on to that bus there. You're here, first and fore-most, to play football, and secondly to clean up.' Chris turned out to be one of the finest servants ever, a brilliant full back with a fantastic goal-scoring record.

Tommy Smith had been playing for his school team and we wanted him. His mother brought him down to the ground one day and said, 'This is Tommy. He has lost his father. Look after him.'

I said, 'You leave him here, Mrs Smith.' That's how Tommy came, and he has been a tremendous player. From the start he was ambitious and arrogant. He had the right temperament. He was only about sixteen when he played for the reserves at right half against Manchester City. Johnny Morrissey, a cunning player, easy to find, was at outside left, and I told Tommy, who was a good kicker of a ball, that Johnny would be lying deep and he should hit balls across for him. 'When they are all down at your end, Tommy, they are all encroaching this side and leaving Johnny clear,' I said. So Tommy slashed the ball across the face of the pitch and Johnny cut City to pieces. We beat them 6–0.

Tommy made his first team debut against Anderlecht at Anfield in November 1964. It was the first night of the big European games and you could feel the heat in the air. Anderlecht was filled with Belgian international players, and I had seen the Belgian team give England an exhibition at Wembley. It was 2–2, but the score was a farce. Belgium had murdered England. When I came out of the ground I said to Joe Mercer, 'Christ Almighty, how do you beat these?' But when I got back to Liverpool I played all that down of course. I said I didn't rate the Belgians.

Paul Van Himst had torn big Maurice Norman to ribbons at Wembley so, when we had finished a meal at a little hotel outside Liverpool before the game, I said I would play Tommy with ten on his back, defensively, and I would give Gordon Milne the specific job of marking Van Himst when they had the ball. 'When we have the ball, come out and play it, Gordon, then pick him up wherever he goes,' I said. They had a defender to mark Tommy, who was sweeping up with Ronnie Yeats. Milne revelled in his job. He might have scored three or four goals that night.

We beat Anderlecht 3–0 in Liverpool and 1–0 in Brussels to

go through to the quarter-finals of the European Cup. Helenio Herrera, of Inter-Milan, was there watching us, and we frightened him. He said he wanted to keep away from Liverpool.

The only time Chris Lawler was injured was when Tommy Smith 'did' him in a five-a-side match at Melwood. We had just got the pitch levelled and Tommy, who was younger than Chris, caught him with the sole of his boot. Chris's ankle went up like a balloon, but he was only out of action for ten days.

It was around the time we were due to play Anderlecht and one day we were playing a five-a-side game and Chris, still injured, was watching. The boys called Chris 'Silent Knight' because he had so little to say for himself. My team in the five-a-side was claiming a goal and I said, 'Just hold on, Chris, you were watching.'

'Yes,' he said.

'Speak up, Chris,' I said, 'I can't hear you. Did you think that was a goal, Chris?'

'No,' he said.

'Good God, Chris,' I said, 'this is the first time I've heard you speak to me and you tell me a bloody lie!'

Chris was unshakeable, you see. I don't know whether he took it badly or took it well, but it caused a good laugh.

So we were building up all the time, becoming more formidable through experience. In 1963 we bought Peter Thompson from Preston for £32,000, and Thompson became one of the greatest Liverpool players. He came from Carlisle, and in fact I was manager at Carlisle when Peter went to Preston as a schoolboy.

He was strong, fast and elusive, and the damage he did was unbelievable. It was indirect more than direct damage. He made people twist and turn and run back. He would turn players around down the left side of the field and then he would switch over and turn them round down the right. In the end he would have all the opposition players running towards their own goal. They would not be playing against us at all! Then, on the right, Ian Callaghan would be doing the same thing. The opposition was frightened to play offside because Peter might burst through and leave them standing. Peter did not score as many goals as he might have done, because he had a tremendous shot in either foot, but what a lot of people couldn't see was the way he created so many openings for the other players by turning the opposition inside out.

Even with the right players and the right training, your plans can fall down because of injuries, so when we heard about a treatment machine that could cut down drastically on the time it took to get a man fit again and back in the team, we decided we must have it. My brother Bob, in Dundee, told me about the machine. He had heard about it from an osteopath. It was invented by an Austrian called Dr Nemec, and it had taken him twenty-five years to perfect it. The beauty of the machine was that not only was it so effective, it was also portable, so we could take it with us on the coach or even on the train and treat injured players right up to kick-off time even when we were playing away from home.

The trouble was in locating Dr Nemec. We searched for him all over Europe until, at last, we heard he was in Liechtenstein and I wrote to him there and he told us where we could get hold of one of his machines. We also found out there was a man in Birmingham who could service it, so he took it at the end of each season so it would be ready for action again as soon as the players came back from the summer break.

When we were developing Melwood I decided against having a place there where the players could eat. I felt it was most important that, after training, the boys should have a cooling-off period before they took a bath and had a meal, and the forty-five minutes between the end of training and arriving back at Anfield was just right. If you have a hot bath when you're perspiring you perspire all day. Our system prevented the players from catching colds and it also made sure that they were not strangers to their home ground.

We were also careful in our choice of playing kit and boots and in having studs to suit all playing conditions, including sets of diced rubber studs for icy pitches. It was no accident that Liverpool came to be noted for strength and fitness. It was due to our attention to detail. We never left anything to chance.

9 Never Walk Alone

The whole of Liverpool came alive in the 1960s, with the Beatles and Cilla Black and comedians like Ken Dodd and Jimmy Tarbuck. The city became world-famous because of the Beatles and other pop groups and the supporters of Liverpool Football Club became world-famous as well. The whole thing was boiling and bubbling and this was what I had been looking for right from the start.

One of the local singers, Gerry Marsden, who was also a Liverpool FC fanatic, made a recording of the song 'You'll Never Walk Alone' and in no time our supporters on the Kop adopted it and sang it, waving their red-and-white scarves in rhythm, wherever the team played. They were a variety turn, and soon their songs and chants were copied by supporters of all the other teams.

Liverpool had never won the FA Cup, and that was a terrible thing, but the fervour and humour of our supporters came over loud and clear at Wembley in 1965. They even changed the National Anthem to 'God Save Our Gracious Team' – and that was the finest I ever heard the anthem sung! At the end of the day they chanted, 'Ee-aye-addio, we've won the Cup!'

It was a wet day, raining and splashing, and my shoes and pants were covered in white from the chalk off the pitch as I walked up to the end of the ground where our supporters were massed. We had beaten Leeds United and our players had the arena, but I took off my coat and went to the supporters because they had got the Cup for the first time.

Grown men were crying and it was the greatest feeling any human being could have to see what we had done. There have been many proud moments. Wonderful, fantastic moments. But that was the greatest day.

We were determined to do everything in our power to make sure nothing went wrong for us. In fact we even went to the extent of having an empty bus follow us to Wembley from our hotel in Weybridge, just in case there was a breakdown on the way.

There was no doubt in our minds. We thought we were a better team than Leeds, much better, and we could have gone out and tried to go after them. But Leeds were cagey and we took our time. We knew we had plenty of that. The rain was belting down and the grass was thick, heavy to play on, so we decided we would not take too much out of ourselves. We would play the ball around and be patient. We were not going to be erratic. We wanted to win that Cup. Whether we entertained people or not didn't make any difference. In the end we had to go into extra time, but we won the game.

Injury kept Gordon Milne from the final and after just three minutes of the game Gerry Byrne, our left back, broke a collarbone in a tackle with Bobby Collins. We didn't know whether to shift him or leave him where he was. I recalled a match at Blackpool when I was a Preston player. Andy Beattie strained a muscle and I said, 'Just leave it, Andy. Play behind me, you might not get anything to do.' Andy had nothing to do, got through the match, and we won. If he had gone to outside right or outside left, the opposition would have known he was injured. So we did the same with Gerry Byrne. We didn't give our hand away. We let it go. Gerry's bones were grinding together, but he stuck it out and should have had all the medals to himself.

St John scored the goal, which made him a hero for all time. We celebrated with a banquet at the Hilton and brought the Cup into the city of Liverpool from Lime Street Station. That was a mistake. We should have left the train at Allerton, as we did when we won the Cup in 1974, and driven the rest of the way into the city by bus so that more people could have seen the Cup on the outskirts. But the reception in the city centre was unbelievable. The emotion was tremendous. When we came out of the station we couldn't see anything but buildings and faces. People were climbing up the walls of shops and banks and hoardings to get a better view. They were in dangerous places. But their name was on the Cup at last, and that was all that mattered.

That was only the beginning really. We won the League championship again the next season and we would have won it again the season after that if we had been able to get hold of one or two players who became available around that time. We were a bit unlucky once or twice in having players lined up but not getting them. But many things happen in football.

Because of our fitness and the pressure we put upon the opposition, the teams we built came to be called 'Powerhouse'. We were strong, that's true, but we didn't get the credit we deserved for the skill in the team. Ronnie Yeats was a big fellow, but he had skill. Gerry Byrne was a great football player. Chris Lawler had class and so did Tommy Smith. Willie Stevenson was a wonderful passer of a ball. Peter Thompson was tricky. Ian St John was crafty and cunning. Ian Callaghan was clever, and so was Roger Hunt. Geoff Strong, whom I bought from Arsenal for £40,000 in 1964, the year we sold Jimmy Melia to Wolves, was good enough to play in any position, and only injuries robbed Alf Arrowsmith of a great career as a goal-taker.

They played brilliant games against the great teams of Anderlecht, Inter-Milan and Tottenham. We beat Wolves 6–0 one day at Wolverhampton and in the closing stages we hit the post three or four times. It was unbelievable the shellacking we gave to that team.

People said we were mechanical, though 'methodical' would have been a better word. At least we knew what we were doing. They said we were predictable. Well, I think anybody who is unpredictable is a waste of time. Being predictable is not too bad. Joe Louis was predictable. He would knock men down on the floor. Goodbye! We were predictable, but the opposition couldn't

stop us. 'Their defence is square and vulnerable,' they would say
– no wonder we let in twenty-four goals in two separate seasons!

We were methodical and precise. We knew our strengths and
weaknesses and played to our strengths. That is how we won the
League championship one season using only fourteen players,
giving Bobby Graham a game in the last match of the season.
Everything was planned. The reserve team played like the first
team. Everyone had a job to do. They knew what that job was,
and that made it easier for them.

Our players worked for each other, not for individual honours,
and by working unselfishly they still won the glory of being
selected for international matches. Everyone at the ground
worked for a common cause. The manager trusted the players
and the players trusted the manager.

Herrera knew what we were capable of. He thought we were
the best team in Europe and he knew what he was talking about;
he knew the game. He struck me as a remarkable little fellow, a
cut-throat man who wanted to win. Inter-Milan beat Rangers
on aggregate that season, though Rangers won 1–0 in the game
at Ibrox in March 1965. Herrera said afterwards, 'If we had
played Liverpool that night we would have been thrashed.'

I thought we should have been the first English club to win the
European Cup. We were good enough to beat Anderlecht home
and away and we had got through against Cologne on the toss
of a coin, after the third game between us had been drawn 2–2
in Rotterdam following scoreless draws on our ground and theirs.
And we had gone from there to reach Wembley by beating
Chelsea and had won the FA Cup. Three days after Wembley
we thrashed Inter-Milan, who were the champions of the world,
3–1 at Anfield in the semi-final of the European Cup.

We were without Gerry Byrne as well as Gordon Milne that
night, but though they were missing from the team because of
injuries, they still played their part. I asked Milan to go out
early, but they kept hanging about the dressing-room. I said,
'It's time to go now,' and eventually they made a move and went
out on to the pitch. That's just what I wanted, psychologically,

because I then sent out Gordon and Gerry with the FA Cup, followed by the team.

Dear God, what an eruption there was when our supporters caught sight of that Cup. The noise was unbelievable. The people were hysterical.

Herrera had been over two or three times to see us, but he had not seen us play the way we did that night and he gave us credit for it afterwards. 'We have been beaten before,' he said, 'but tonight we were defeated.' Milan were technically sound, but we beat them. Roger Hunt hit the ball when he was about four feet in the air to score one of the goals. He hooked it and slashed it into the net. 'That was not a British goal,' Herrera said. 'It was a Continental goal.'

But the second leg of the semi-final was not a game, it was a war. We stayed at Lake Como, and we had trouble with the church bells. It wasn't so bad until about eleven o'clock at night, when the noise of the day had ceased and there was nothing to hear but the bells. One in particular was like doomsday.

Bob Paisley and I went to see the Monsignor about it. We tried to get him to stop the bells ringing for the night so the players could sleep. 'It's not very fair,' I said to him through an interpreter. 'We didn't know about this noise and we've come here on the eve of the most important match in the world this year, Inter-Milan versus Liverpool.' That was right, because if we had won it, we would have won the European Cup.

He was sympathetic towards us, but he said he could not do what we asked. So I said, 'Well, could you let Bob here go up and put a bandage on them and maybe kind of dull them a bit?' Crepe bandages and cotton-wool! Bob was killing himself laughing. That would have been one of the funniest things Bob had ever done, one of his greatest cures as a trainer, creeping up the aisle with cotton-wool and bandages! But we just had to put up with the noise.

There was no joy in the match at the San Siro stadium in Milan. The Milan supporters had been told that the fans at Anfield had been like animals because of the noise they had made when Milan had been sent out first and we then brought out the FA Cup. But what did they expect? We had got the Cup for the first time and it was the greatest night of their lives. The crowd in the San Siro was really hostile. They even had smoke bombs, purple things in jars that went up in smoke when they burst. One of these landed on the steps and Bob Paisley's clothes were covered in the stuff.

Inter beat us 3–0 but not even their players enjoyed the game, and we didn't think two of the goals were legal. They put an indirect free kick straight into the net for the first, and the ball was kicked out of Tommy Lawrence's hands before the second. Afterwards the people were sweeping the streets with enormous flags and I said to our players, 'All right, we've lost. But see what you have done. Inter-Milan are the unofficial champions of the world and all these people are going mad because they are so pleased that they have beaten Liverpool. That's the standard you have raised yourselves up to.'

The following season, 1965–66, we won the League championship again and reached the final of the European Cup-winners' Cup, beating Juventus, Standard-Liège, Honved, and Celtic in the semi-finals. We ended the season at Hampden Park in May in the final against Borussia Dortmund. It was a wet night and I felt that the Germans were a little bit chary of us and afraid of the reputations of the Scottish supporters and the Liverpool supporters. But they beat us 2–1 in extra time and, having already won the League, that was a big disappointment for us. It would have been nice to have won a trophy back home in Scotland on top of everything else.

Hampden was in a bad condition that night and the attendance wasn't very high. The fact that we had beaten Celtic may have disappointed some Scottish supporters. It is no good complaining. We didn't play well and we gave away two silly goals. The Germans got the breaks and that was it. That's what football is all about.

Roger Hunt scored our goal and had a chance to win the game for us, but he was handicapped by an ankle injury and was not at his best. It was hurting him too much and he just couldn't manage a telling shot. Roger would never shirk anything. He was a great player with a big heart who was hell-bent on scoring goals. He was not afraid to try shots, and that is what scoring is all about. Some players shy at them, they don't want chances. But Roger was always hungry for them.

To offset losing that final, we had the championship, which put us into the European Cup again in 1966–67. Petrolul Ploesti, of Rumania, took us to three matches in the first round, but we beat them 2–0 in the play-off in Brussels. Then we came up against Ajax, of Amsterdam.

Ajax had the makings of a team then, but they were not yet the great team that they later became. We played them first in Amsterdam, but the match should never have started. The fog was terrible. We were due to play Manchester United at Old Trafford the following Saturday, and that was a vital game for us. We didn't want to be delayed in Amsterdam, playing on Thursday and not returning home until the Friday. But it was not our decision to go ahead with the match. Leo Horne, the observer for UEFA, European football headquarters, was responsible for that.

The referee, an Italian, said, 'If we can see from goal to goal, OK. If not, no game.'

Leo Horne said, 'No. In Holland, if we can see from the half-way line to goal, we play.'

So the game was played. We couldn't see much of the game at all, sitting on the sidelines. We couldn't even see the ball. But the pressmen reported it in full!

We were 2–0 down and Willie Stevenson and Geoff Strong started raiding. They were stung and went mad and tried to retrieve the game. So I went on to the pitch while the game was in progress and was walking about in the fog, and I said to Willie and Geoff, 'Christ, this is only the first game. There's another bloody game at Liverpool, so don't go and give away more goals. Let's get beat 2–0. We are not doing too bad. Take it easy.'

I walked on to the pitch, talked to the players, and walked off again – and the referee never saw me!

We lost 5–1, but I still thought we could get through at Anfield. Candidly, I thought that at our best we might have beaten them

6–0, and I said so. We drew 2–2 at Liverpool. Cruyff was only a youngster then, of course, but he scored both goals. We threw everything to the winds and they were lucky to get a draw near the end. We should have won the second game, but Peter Thompson hit the post three times in about ten minutes.

We were out of Europe again, but we were undeterred. We were too busy to let set-backs like that bother us. We were examining the team and planning ahead.

10 The New Team

We had a mediocre time for a while in the late 1960s as we prepared for the 1970s. A lot of our players were about the same age
and I had given them a set time as to how long I thought they
would last. I had told them, 'If you are a good athlete, your best
seasons will be between twenty-eight and thirty-three. I had my
best seasons during that period of my life.'

I thought some of them would have gone on longer than they
did, because of their experience. Maybe the success they had
shortened their careers. They had won the League, the FA Cup
and the League again, and they had been in Europe so often.
They had played everybody and had done most things. Perhaps
they were no longer hungry enough.

The search for players had never ceased of course. In 1967
we bought Tony Hateley from Chelsea for £96,000 because he
was brilliant in the air and looked as if he was going to be the
answer to everything. He started off well, a bright, likeable lad
with a good personality. The crowd took to him immediately,
and he responded to them. But things did not break for Tony.
He had a string of injuries – his injury sheet was frightening –
and they took the sting out of him. It was difficult to get front
men, and a fit Tony Hateley was worth his weight in gold. In
the circumstances, Tony did well for us, but we transferred him
to Coventry for £80,000 after about a year.

We had been unlucky with some of the players already on our

books. Alf Arrowsmith, playing up front with Roger Hunt, with St John a little way behind them, was causing a lot of trouble to defences until injuries lessened his effectiveness. And Gordon Wallace was the nearest thing to Tommy Finney since the war, but Gordon had no luck whatsoever. He had cartilage trouble, arm trouble – Wallace had everything. He played in a League match at Burnley one night when Roger Hunt was injured. We won 3–0 and, honestly, we didn't miss Roger. Gordon played against Birmingham at Anfield and, with about twenty minutes to go, I shut my eyes and thought, 'God, Tommy Finney must be here.' Wallace was beating people in the six-yard box. He was kidding on that he was going to kick the ball and then dribbling past them. He was a real menace.

In September 1968 I paid £100,000 to Wolves for Alun Evans when he was eighteen years old. Alun weighed about eleven and a half stone and was strong. He had been to Anfield with Wolves as a sixteen-year-old and had given Ronnie Yeats a hard time. He had scored a goal that day and showed he had everything necessary to be a great player. He had all the essentials, all the skill. He was cute for his age, backing into people and getting fouls awarded against them. He was quick and courageous.

Alun was refreshing. The first match he played in we scored four goals against Leicester, and Alun scored one of them. The following week we went to Wolverhampton and beat them 6–0, with Alun scoring two of the goals. We scored six and hit the post and crossbar three times as well. The Wolverhampton people were wishing the final whistle would blow. I heard one say afterwards. 'Thank God that's over.'

After the match I told Alun, 'Don't say anything, son. Don't say anything to anyone about Wolverhampton Wanderers. Don't be going to the newspaper-men and talking about this and that and saying Wolves made a mistake in selling you and all that kind of thing, because that can blow back in your face.' I wanted the lad to keep his feet on the ground.

Everything was going well for Alun until he went home one weekend. Apparently he was sitting in a night-club when there was an incident. He was hit in the face with a glass and very badly cut.

That incident possibly changed Alun's whole life. His face was badly scarred and that was embarrassing for the boy. He had great spirit, but what happened retarded his career. Everything seemed to go wrong for him afterwards. He had to have a cartilage operation after being injured on a bone-hard pitch when we played a European match in Bucharest and he continued to have set-backs. He was the victim of circumstances to a certain extent. Liverpool were bursting for success and what happened to Alun could just as easily have happened to someone else. Anybody could have been in the same position and have been out. We transferred him to Aston Villa, which meant he was going back home, and it suited him.

Sometimes when a player leaves a club there are sour grapes. Maybe the manager was to blame, maybe the player, and so on. Things did not work out too well for Alun at Liverpool, but not long ago I received a letter from him. It began : 'Dear Boss . . .'

Alun was having a little bit of difficulty at the time and wrote to me for advice. It was touch-and-go what he would do about his future and I spoke to the boy on the phone. Since then he has moved on to Walsall.

I was very pleased and proud that Alun had come to me for advice. That letter meant a lot to me. And let me make one point quite clear. I paid £100,000 for Alun Evans when he was eighteen – and I would do the same thing all over again.

There was also the case of Ted MacDougall. Ted had been transferred to York City for £5500 in 1966, but when Ted was on our books there were a lot of good forwards ahead of him and he couldn't get a game in the first team. He promised well and we took him to Villa Park one day as substitute. But we had so many good players at that particular time that we felt we could afford to let Ted go. 'You can go to York if you want to, son,' I told him – I never told players, 'Look, somebody is after you and you should go' – and Ted moved on. He has done well, and I'm glad, because he's a dangerous player and a genuine boy.

I saw Emlyn Hughes play his first game for Blackpool in the

last game of the 1965–66 season. It was at Blackburn Rovers' ground. Blackpool had escaped relegation and Blackburn had gone down. Matt Busby was at that game and it was rumoured that he was after Mike England. I said to Ronnie Suart, the Blackpool manager, 'Who's playing?' and he said, 'There is a boy here from Barrow in his first game.'

Emlyn had played in all positions in the junior teams at Blackpool without causing any eyes to flicker and Ronnie said, 'We're playing him tonight at left back.' He didn't half play! He did everything – even to the extent of getting a player sent off. The player retaliated against Emlyn, who was in the right, and I thought, 'That will upset him.' But it didn't. He kept on playing and was cutting inside, and cutting the ball back out.

I offered £25,000 for him right after the match. He had played only one game and all the Blackpool directors were sitting puffing cigars because they had escaped relegation. I thought, 'I'll get this player because they'll be feeling kind-hearted.' I should have said, 'You should thank your lucky stars. Let us have him. You've got something – give something to somebody else!'

Unfortunately for us, Blackpool sold Alan Ball to Everton the following summer and were not in any great hurry for more money. Otherwise I would have had Emlyn sooner. But I had cottoned on to him from the beginning, when I had said to myself, 'This is somebody special,' and I had been following him. Among my letters at the time were a number from a man from the Fylde, who kept writing to tell me, 'Emlyn Hughes is going to be a good player.' He didn't know I knew that already.

I started off the next season looking at Emlyn again, and in a match against Chelsea, when Tommy Docherty was the manager, Emlyn and Peter Osgood had a set-to. Emlyn nipped Peter in a tackle, and in the next tackle Peter tried to 'do' Emlyn, but Emlyn was either lucky or cute and broke Peter's leg, unfortunately. I still think that Peter was as much responsible for it as Emlyn. Anyway, I followed the boy and I was more convinced than ever that I wanted him, and eventually I got him for £65,000 in February 1967, when he was nineteen. Emlyn was one of the **major signings of all time.**

As soon as we had sorted things out we went to Emlyn's digs for his belongings and then drove him to Liverpool. On the way another car ran into the back of mine and smashed one of the rear lights. I got out and said to the driver, 'What the bloody hell do you think you're doing?' Before he could answer, I told him, 'Never mind, it's only a rear light – I've got what I want in the car.' A bit further on I was stopped by a policeman, who said, 'You've only got one rear light.' I said, 'I know, a fellow's just driven into the back of me. Give me a chance to get to a garage for God's sake.' We arrived back without incident after that.

The following summer we toured Germany and Emlyn gave Overath a mauling in Cologne. Emlyn was given a roving commission, like the one we gave Gordon Milne against Van Himst at his best. I said to Emlyn, 'Now, Overath is a good player, son,' and he was. He was promising to be one of the best in the world. 'You just mark Overath,' I said. 'Don't be negative all the time. When we get the ball, play with it, and when they get it, pick up Overath again.'

So Overath was being shadowed by Emlyn and was not getting a kick of the ball. Emlyn had a tackle on him and Overath went over the top of the ball at him and Emlyn had a little kick at him, a little flick. The referee was coming across and we were going to have a player sent off in a friendly match.

Immediately, Bob Paisley went over to Emlyn, while I said to Geoff Strong, one of the substitutes, 'Come on, Geoff, just go on.' So Geoff trotted on to the field with me, and Bob, who is cute, told Emlyn to lie down.

'Stretcher! Stretcher!' shouted Bob, who knew Emlyn had got the ticket.

I said to Geoff, 'You warm up, and when Emlyn is on the stretcher, you take his place.'

So Emlyn went on the stretcher – nothing wrong with him, of course – and went off to nice polite applause and Geoff went on to the field.

But Overath said to the referee, 'The substitute . . .'

And the referee said to Geoff, 'Nein, nein, nein – Off! Off!'

Bob and I nearly got Geoff on, and I said to Overath, 'It's a friendly match. People are paying two pounds to see it. Do you want us to play with ten men?'

'No speak English. No speak English,' he said. But he could speak English.

'Listen, Overath, you can bloody well speak English. Don't come that stuff with me,' I said.

So I went up to the stand to see the president of Cologne, a Mr Kramer, a tycoon, who was wearing a big red tie. 'Mr Kramer,' I said, 'we beat you on the toss of a coin in Rotterdam, and you are trying to get your own back. There's a bloody player been sent off in a friendly match. You have got the authority to go down at half-time and say, "Put somebody else on or put the boy back on." If you don't want to put the boy back on, let's have another player on. You are depriving the crowd of entertainment. People have paid two pounds and we are playing with only ten men.'

'Very difficult,' he said.

'No, it is not difficult at all,' I said. 'We could pack up now. We could say, "No, Mr Kramer, sorry, we are not playing any more. Bugger you." '

'Oh, no,' he replied.

I said, 'There is only one thing I need to do now, Mr Kramer. I'll get Tommy Smith to injure one of your players and that will level the game up!' and left it at that. Funnily enough, we went on to Hanover, and Tommy had a few of them crippled. He had three of them limping at the back of the goal all at one time, and the referee came to me at half-time and said, 'Number ten, Schmidt. Take it easy. I send him off.'

'Schmidt?' I said. 'Schmidt is a German. Do you want Mr Smith or Messerschmitt?'

So we had Emlyn, and the search continued. I couldn't go out and buy £100,000 players and put them in the reserves, so we started scouring the lower divisions. In between times we sold Gordon Milne to Blackpool for £50,000 and Willie Stevenson to Stoke for £50,000.

I would think about the players we had and I could see that some of them were going a bit. When you have had success it can be a difficult job to motivate yourself. You have done it before, like walking up and down the same road all the time. I felt that was happening to some of the players.

The breaking-up process started at Watford, where we lost an FA Cup-tie. That was the crucial game. Peter Thompson and Tommy Smith didn't play. If they had, Watford could not have beaten us, because in actual fact I thought Peter and Tommy could have beaten Watford by themselves! Like the joke about Charlie Tully being the only Celtic player to turn up to play Rangers one day. So Charlie played them on his own in the first half and it was no score. The rest of the Celtic team turned up for the second half, and Rangers won. If Peter and Tommy had played Watford by themselves they might have given them a hard game. And if we had beaten Watford it would possibly have been a different story.

I had vouched for that team. There had been games during which I hadn't batted an eyelid. I knew we would win. It was just a question of how long it would take and how many we would score. Sometimes Tommy Lawrence would play a whole game and never touch the ball. Now it was obvious that while some of the players still had an appetite for success, others hadn't and might do better elsewhere.

After Watford I knew I had to do my job and change my team. I had a duty to perform for myself, my family, Liverpool Football Club and the supporters, who had been used to success after our winning the Second Division championship, the First Division championship, the FA Cup, the championship again, and reaching the semi-final of the European Cup and the final of the Cupwinners' Cup. It had to be done, and if I didn't do it I was shirking my obligations.

Gerry Byrne was forced to pack up because of injury and now I had to leave out men like Tommy Lawrence, Ronnie Yeats, Roger Hunt and Ian St John. Chris Lawler, Tommy Smith, Peter Thompson and Ian Callaghan were young enough to go on. Geoff Strong – the unluckiest man not to have a regular place in the team and not to play for England – was still able to play a Bobby Moore sweeper role in an armchair, Bobby Graham did a tremendous job for us until he broke an ankle, and we had Emlyn. So we had to fill in the blanks.

That first team we had at Liverpool was lauded as the greatest and songs were made up about the players. They were worth it. They were the fellows who made Liverpool Football Club what it is today. But the show had to go on.

Gradually we were bringing players into the team. Some of them already had a couple of Central League championship medals before they got a chance in the big time. I could afford to buy players in their teens from the lower divisions and prepare them for a couple of years in the reserves.

One of these players was Ray Clemence. I watched Ray more often than any other player I bought, because he was a goal-keeper. I used to travel to see him at Scunthorpe, where they kicked off at a quarter to seven on Friday night every fortnight, and I spoke to other managers about him.

When you go to see a goalkeeper, he might never get a cross to cut out. The next time he might not have a shot to stop. And you also go to check on the little things, like the way he kicks the ball. That is why I watched Ray so often.

He is left-footed, and I thought, 'I hope he is not left-handed.' I don't like left-footed goalkeepers, especially if they are left-handed as well. I'm not suggesting they aren't good enough, but I have always felt they are short of balance. Ray was left-footed but right-handed, and that was good. We signed him for £18,000 on a Saturday afternoon during the summer of 1967.

We were adding to our strength all the time, signing Alec Lindsay from Bury for £67,000 and Larry Lloyd from Bristol Rovers for £50,000 in 1969. It took a while before Alec realized his true potential and found his best position, left back. Alec could play with style and cross the ball with pin-point accuracy into the penalty area with his left foot, and he went on to play for England. Larry Lloyd was recommended to me by Freddie Ford, who was one of my trainers when I was manager of Carlisle. Freddie was then with Bristol Rovers, and I watched Larry play in a cup-tie against Everton at Goodison Park. He was big and strong. I bought John Toshack from Cardiff City for

£111,000 in 1970. John, a wonderful header of a ball, had outgrown his strength, but he had scored a lot of goals for Cardiff and his tremendous potential was obvious. With Liverpool, he became stronger and always made his contribution to the team's success. His most effective performances came after his transfer from Liverpool to Leicester City for £160,000 was cancelled on medical grounds in November 1974. I had left by then, of course, but I think John was riled that Liverpool were ready to let him go and so he proved himself in the best possible way, producing the form I knew he was capable of when I bought him. In 1970, we also introduced two university graduates, Brian Hall, who had come up through the reserves, and Steve Heighway, from Skelmersdale United. Brian studied at Liverpool University while he was coming up through our reserve team and it must have been very difficult for him. He is small, but full of tricks: a crafty player. I went to Warwickshire to interview Steve when he was still at university down there, and he made a dramatic move from non-League football to the First Division.

Another important addition had yet to arrive, of course.

11 A Boy Called Keegan

Kevin Keegan came to the notice of Liverpool Football Club through Andy Beattie, the same Andy Beattie who was my team-mate at Preston and asked me to join him as his assistant at Huddersfield, where I succeeded him as manager. Andy came to work for me as a part-time scout for a while after he had left another club, and the first thing he said to me when he arrived was, 'There is a boy at Scunthorpe. He is about eighteen. I have been watching him now for nine months. I think he has tremendous potential and I can't understand why nobody has gone for him.'

Things like that surprise me. Andy kept recommending this boy to a club. He was watched, but not signed. (A more recent case is the winger Gordon Hill, of Manchester United. How the people in London missed him I don't know. They must have gone to the games wearing dark glasses.)

So Andy drummed this boy's name into me and everybody on our training and coaching staff saw him play. By this time other clubs were interested in him, of course, and he played at Goodison Park one night. Eventually, I decided to sign him. I had to, because Andy was so sure about Kevin.

It was near the end of the season and we were in the 1971 FA Cup Final when we bought Kevin for £35,000. In the end it turned out to be robbery with violence, but we did not know that then. Later you could argue that Scunthorpe should have got another £100,000 after the way this boy turned out.

We were in the Cup Final and the place was alive when Kevin arrived. He sat on top of a dustbin beside the temporary offices we had at Anfield while the new stand was being fitted out, and it must have seemed that nobody was taking any notice of him. He must have thought, 'Christ, this is a place.' But one fellow was taking notice of him, and that was me. I said, 'Listen, son, you'll get your pants all dirty on that bin. Don't sit on dirty bins.' Maybe Kevin thought he was being shunned, or that we were too big to have time for him because we were in the Final. But I was watching his reactions to what was going on, and the fact that nobody was bothering with him didn't daunt him.

He signed on for wages that weren't very much more than he was getting at Scunthorpe, but I told him, 'It's not the wages that count, son. If I had been given the chance to go to a big club, I would have signed on for that club, and then I would have said, "How much are you paying me?" That was my idea of football and my idea of life – the opportunity to get somewhere. So it's not what you get now, son, it's the opportunity here to win cups, international caps and everything.' This was exactly the advice my brother Alec gave me when I went to Preston for ten shillings more than I was getting at Carlisle. Kevin's next two wages from Liverpool were doubled and doubled again. By this time he had got three trophies and was playing for England.

He came, and we took him with us to the Cup Final against Arsenal. When we lost he looked broken-hearted and I thought, 'Christ, here is a real character – and he is not even playing. He probably thinks that if he had been playing we would have won.' And we would have done!

At the start of the following season he wanted to be bloody first at everything in training – sprinting, jumping over the hurdles, playing five-a-sides, everything. He ran his guts out. He had been to weightlifting classes as a boy to develop his shoulders and thighs and calves and, boy, was he keen to be fit.

We went on a pre-season tour abroad, but Kevin stayed behind

E

to train with the reserves because we weren't sure of giving him
a game, and we had arranged for the reserves to play matches
back home. When we came back we had a little bit of doubt up the
front. We weren't really strong enough, to tell you the truth. I
said to Ronnie Moran, who was now the reserve-team trainer,
'The boy, Kevin, how did he do?'

'He's worked hard. He's done well,' said Ronnie. 'He's quick
and strong and fights to win all the time and tries to do everything in a hurry.'

Before the start of the season one of our training functions was
to get balls crossed from left and right for players to slash into
the goal, which was empty apart from the net. They would just
batter the ball from about twelve yards. And who sent the ball
ripping into the net most? Kevin Keegan – Woof! Woof! Woof!
Right, left and centre.

The Tuesday morning before the season started we had a
full-scale practice match and I stuck the boy into the team.
Normally matches between the first team and the reserves are
stalemate. The purpose of the games is to get players fit, not to
see who wins and who loses, because the players know each
other so well that they cancel each other out. I always stressed
to the players that it didn't matter who won and who lost these
games – because if the reserve team beats the first team it doesn't
leave a good taste.

Kevin was in the first team that morning and they scored
seven goals, which was unusual, to say the least. Kevin was playing against Ian Ross, who did wonderful jobs for us sweeping
up at centre back or marking players like Alan Ball and Franz
Beckenbauer – I once sent him upfield to watch Beckenbauer
and he looked a good centre forward! So I had a quiet word
with Ian, who is a genuine boy. 'What's going on?' I said. 'What
about it, son?'

He said, 'Ah . . . this boy.'

'That's the difference between the team before and the team
now?' I asked.

'Yes,' he said, 'he's a hell of a hard boy to tab. He's twisting
and turning.'

I said, 'I know, I saw it. I saw the trouble he was causing. I just wanted to know from a player like you, who has been able to tab great players like Alan Ball. The boy Keegan gave you a drubbing, didn't he?'

'Yes,' he said, 'he's very quick and you don't know what he's going to do.'

We were due to play Nottingham Forest at home in the first game of the season and I had a problem position at the front of the team. Late in the week I saw Kevin upstairs in the big room at Anfield where the guests in the directors' box go for refreshments.

'Excuse me a minute, son, how are you feeling?' I said.

'Oh, I'm fit,' he said. 'I've never trained like that. I've had five weeks of it, and I've never trained like that.'

'Is this the fittest you have been?' I asked.

'Oh, yes,' he said.

He was a shy boy, and I said, 'Would you like to play in the team.'

'Oh yes, I would like to play in the team,' he replied.

'Right,' I said, 'you are playing on Saturday in the First Division.'

He played, scored a goal, and caused a bit of havoc.

Kevin's whole world had changed. He was in the big league and was doing well. Then he developed a sore foot. He complained about pain in the bony part of the foot.

'It's terrible. I can hardly walk,' he said.

'At your age!' I said. 'In the bony part of your foot! Listen, son, if you had come in at Preston and said you had a sore foot you would have got shot. So get out and train and bloody play.'

He said, 'You don't believe me!'

His foot was sore, but he was sore as well, and he was arguing with Bob and Joe and me, and again I thought, 'Well, here's a character.' I was reading him.

'I believe you,' I said. 'What's up with your foot? What's made it sore?'

His car was mentioned.

'What's up with your car?' I said.

'Oh, the clutch is stiff.'

I said to Joe Fagan, 'Joe, go out and try his clutch, will you?'

Joe, who is a big fellow, came back and said, 'I can't push it in. I can't push the bloody thing in!'

Kevin had been pushing the flesh of his foot on to the bone and making himself crippled with that clutch. I told him, 'Get rid of the car until the clutch gets sorted out, or get a new car.'

That was how we paid attention to detail. He stopped driving that car and stopped driving altogether for a while until his foot was better.

Kevin proved to be one of the best players in Britain. He is the best forward in England, but I don't like to distinguish between the players I had. There were so many: Gerry Byrne, who was on the transfer list when I came, a brilliant player; Chris Lawler, the ground-staff boy who trained at night until I put that right, and who became one of the great full backs; Tommy Smith, who wanted to be in the team when he was sixteen; Ian St John and Ronnie Yeats, who were the foundations of Liverpool – never mind anybody else! And there was Roger Hunt, who drew admiration from me the moment I saw him; and the brilliant Peter Thompson, ravishing the opposition – never mind about him not scoring as many goals as he should or talking about his final pass, because that's all crap. Ian Callaghan, another brilliant boy, was an example to everyone; and there was Emlyn Hughes – wonderful! fantastic! – who was bought at a time when others were waning; and Ray Clemence, who cost even less than Kevin and who became the best goalkeeper in the world and was in the team that repeated the Tommy Lawrence record of conceding only twenty-four goals in forty-two games. (In fact Ray conceded only twenty-two in forty-one matches, because we played the reserve team at Maine Road one night and drew 2–2 and got fined £7000 by the League.)

But, by virtue of having come from the Fourth Division – from that class of football – and having been chucked straight into the first team and done so well, whereas the others either came from good-class football or were tried in the reserves first,

Kevin heads the list. Not that I am going to say he is better than all the others, but he was thrown into the fire and he ignited the new team. He brought it to life with awareness and skill.

He was the inspiration of the new team.

12 Triumph Again

My biggest thrill as a player was winning the FA Cup with Preston. My greatest day in football was when Liverpool won the FA Cup for the first time. But winning the League Championship for the third time, and with a brand new team, possibly gave me more satisfaction than anything. By achieving that, Liverpool equalled Arsenal's record of eight championships – and that same season, 1972–73, we brought home a European trophy, the UEFA Cup.

The policy of the new team was the same as that of the old. We played to our strengths. We pressurized everybody and made them run. We didn't concede many goals and perhaps we didn't score as many goals as we should have done, because we had the opposition back defending and blocking up their goal. The more players there are in the penalty box – even your own players – the more difficult it can be to score goals.

We had devised a system of play which minimized the risk of injuries. The team played in sections of the field, like a relay. We didn't want players running the length of the field, stretching themselves unnecessarily, so our back men played in one area, and then passed on to the midfield men, in their area, and so on to the front men. So, whilst there was always room for individuals within our system, the work was shared out. It was no accident that during my time at Anfield eight players played more than three hundred League matches – Ian Callaghan 502, Chris

Lawler 396, Roger Hunt 384, Peter Thompson 377, Tommy Smith 367, Ron Yeats 359, Ian St John 335 and Tommy Lawrence 305. Emlyn Hughes, who had played 264 League matches during my time, is now well past the 300 mark and Ray Clemence, Kevin Keegan and Steve Heighway are among those well on the way.

We didn't believe in resting players simply because we had a heavy programme of matches. We wouldn't put in young players who were not familiar with the pattern and who would consequently put extra pressure on the rest of the team.

Tony Waiters had joined our training staff for a while, and Tony is a very clever fellow. The initial training before one season, with Tony's ideas, combining with ours, was tremendous. There was so much variation that the time passed quickly, and I have never known so much enjoyment at training. Tony had been all for signing Steve Heighway, and he saw Steve play more than anyone else on our staff. We picked up a few things from Tony and he possibly picked up a few ideas from us. He left us to play in goal for Burnley for a spell and later became manager of Plymouth.

I saw the emotion in players like Kevin Keegan and Emlyn Hughes when they were in tears after we got pipped for the League in 1971–72, Kevin's first season. We lost the League by a point. At Derby, when we were losing 1–0, Kevin was definitely obstructed in the box when their goalkeeper came and 'did' him, but no penalty was given. That would have won the League for us. Sam Longson, the Derby chairman, was at our last game at Arsenal, when we were robbed of a goal. Kevin went through and gave a slanted pass to John Toshack, who rammed the ball into the net. Everybody in the ground thought it was a goal, but it was disallowed for offside. So we finished third, behind Leeds on goal average, to Derby – who were away at some holiday camp abroad. I took encouragement from the fact that we had played so well at Highbury. The new team had emerged, and the following season we won the League with sixty points.

We were still strong on psychology of course. We even had a plaque put over the tunnel that takes the players from the dressing-rooms to the pitch. Our maintenance foreman, Bert Johnson, had it painted, white letters on a red background : THIS IS ANFIELD. A form of intimidation.

Newcastle United came one day and their players were in good spirits. I couldn't understand it, because they never won any games at our ground. Joe Harvey was at the top of the steps leading down to the tunnel and the players were making their way out; John Tudor, Bob Moncur, and the rest. As Malcolm Macdonald came alongside Joe, he pointed at the plaque and said, 'Joe, we are in the right ground.'

I said, 'You'll soon bloody find out you're in the right ground, son!' – only the words were stronger than that.

We beat Newcastle 5–0 that day – and they had never played better. They were the unluckiest team in the world. It could have been five goals each. It was a fantastic game. We played well and they played well, but we got the breaks and they got nothing. Ray Clemence was absolutely brilliant.

Malcolm Macdonald took it very well. He was quoted in the papers as saying how quickly I had replied to what he had said before the game. Malcolm is a likeable chap and I'd have him in my team. He scores goals because he's unafraid and wants chances.

I always liked to see the opposition players when they walked into the ground and down to the dressing-rooms. I would look up the Rothmans book or the *News of the World* football annual to refresh my mind on their first names, though I knew most of them of course. I would be ready for them when they arrived. I'd say things like, 'Hello, Jimmy, it's a little bit heavy, but it's not a bad ground. In actual fact, it's the kind of ground that suits us. We like to play in certain conditions and today's conditions are just what we wanted. Our players are just geared for it.'

If it was heavy, if it was dry, if it was frosty – it made no difference. I'd say, 'Just a touch of frost. I remember the last time we played on a frosty pitch – oh, we didn't half play well!'

Then I would go into our dressing-room and say, 'Christ, I've seen them coming in, boys. They've been out on the tiles! Bobby Moore looks older than me! I'm not joking, it's bloody unbelievable to see this. I'll tell you something – they were frightened to death!' I said this about everybody. If it had been Real Madrid I would have said the same.

Ron Greenwood and Bobby Moore were once quoted by a newspaper as saying how difficult it was for some teams to score against West Ham. They mentioned Liverpool as being one of them. Well, we went to play at West Ham the Monday after the start of a season and, about ten minutes into the second half, we scored our fifth goal. I turned to Greenwood and said, 'I'll tell you something, Ron, we've got a chance of winning this game!'

We laid down our plans at the start of the season, the way Tottenham did when they won the double in 1960–61. They had one tactical talk at the beginning of the season, with Danny Blanchflower, John White, Bobby Smith, and all of them, and they didn't need any more talks. If you have a good team, a tactical talk at the start, sorting out all the basics so that you know what you are going to do, is enough – unless your players have bad memories. If things were not going right, I would say to the players, 'We'll need to have another tactical talk – your bloody memories have gone! We had one three years ago, and we'll have to have another!'

The players would usually be in the dressing-room at about two o'clock for a Saturday game. Maybe one or two would leave it a bit later. When I was a player, I used to get ready about fifty minutes before a game. I used to take all day, taking off my clothes and putting on my football jersey, shorts, socks and boots. Then I would sit and relax. If anyone said, 'There's somebody outside looking for you,' I would say, 'I'll see them after the match.' I wasn't bothered about handing out tickets and things like that. When I was in the dressing-room I was finished with everything except the match. If somebody had said, 'Your brother is outside,' I would have said, 'Well, tell him I'll see him next summer.' I would rub myself down and put the bandages on my ankles and take my time.

The Liverpool players would probably chat for a few minutes and start getting ready about forty-five minutes before the game. I hated to see teams rushing at the last minute. That's rubbish.

They should be ready in time, so they can relax. A lot of teams do things a certain way because they are superstitious and always have to rush to do something before they go out. I used to say, 'Well, you are better doing it now than on the field!'

I would patter on about the opposition. I'd say, 'Christ, I've seen that new boy of theirs and I'll tell you something now – he didn't sleep a wink last night! What's more, if you run him around he won't sleep a wink tonight either!'

At Preston I was brought up with a lot of funny fellows, and I was a funny fellow too. The trainer used to get us to start a laugh. We used to tell jokes about the old days, when they played in big boots and long drawers and had drooping moustaches. To have somebody in the dressing room who can crack jokes before the game is very good.

'I've seen their substitute,' I'd tell our players at Liverpool, 'and I hope to Christ he has to go on, because I'm bloody sure he doesn't want to go on!' This would be the banter, and I would encourage players to talk to one another. Some were very quiet of course. Ian Callaghan would sit and say very little, but that didn't stop him from being the hardest working player on the field.

I made it my business to know all about my players. I even knew the colour of their eyes. And I always had a high regard for Ian. One day a man came to see me and asked me if I could recommend one of my players who might be the type to join him in an insurance business, with a view to eventually becoming a partner. Without hesitation I told him, 'Ian Callaghan's your man.' Ian went into insurance and has made a success of it. I could never have recommended the boy too highly.

You have probably heard or read about managers 'lifting' their players, and I'll give you an example of what this means. When Steve Heighway joined Liverpool he was a sensation. His fantastic acceleration murdered the opposition. But after a while he showed little signs of fatigue, so I used the kind of psychology on Steve that I have used on other players.

We were travelling to an away match and I went to Steve and said, 'You're looking a bit tired, son. I think you need a rest.' I let him think that I was going to leave him out of the team, and I could see that he was a bit disappointed. Before we came to the end of the journey, I went back to where Steve was sitting and said, 'Do you want to play, son?'

'Oh, yes,' he said, and his face lit up.

'All right, you're playing,' I said. And he reacted as if I had told him he was making his debut all over again.

On the other side of the coin I once picked up the *Liverpool Echo* one Friday night and saw a headline that said Steve wouldn't be playing in a match the following day. Where the paper got the stuff from I don't know, but I thought, 'Christ, the boy will have the paper.'

Straight away, I telephoned Steve's house and said, 'Have you seen the paper, Steve?'

'Yes,' he said.

'Well, it's bloody rubbish, son,' I said. 'Steve Heighway's playing outside left for Liverpool.'

I wasn't going to let the boy go to bed the night before a match thinking he wasn't going to play. I think somebody at the club must have said they didn't think Steve would be playing and it was taken as fact. But only one man picked the team at Liverpool, and that was me.

I would always remind the players not to argue with the referee and I would try to put them at ease a little by saying things like, 'Don't think any individual is expected to win the game by himself. Don't worry that we are depending on you too much. Share out the worries. We're not expecting you, John, to win the game by yourself, or you, Kevin, or anybody. We want all of you to do something. So don't take too much on your plate or put too much in your thoughts and frighten yourself to death. You are as much responsible as the next man for winning, or losing. Don't be impatient. Play together and keep going. Don't be irritated by anybody, and if you are doing what we think is right, never mind about anybody else.'

The plans were laid down and there was very little else you could do – unless by half-time something was very obvious about the opposition. In the days when we had players like St John and

Roger Hunt, we would prime them to try out the opposition. Perhaps a striker would be St John's marker, so we would tell St John to go away somewhere right at the start, to see if his marker would go with him. If he did, we might alter our plans. Those were the days when there was more man-for-man marking. St John would take a walk and the opposing boy would go with him and we would say, 'It's all right, bring him in here and we'll give him some tea!' Roger would take somebody as well and it left a big hole through the middle.

At half-time we might talk about something that was outstanding. These might have been a player who was a bit dodgy on the inside. If it was a full back, I would say, 'Now, you will beat him on the outside, son.' Or, if one of our defenders was playing against a winger who was causing a bit of trouble, we would say, 'Don't let him go down that side, son. Pull him inside. He's hell of a dangerous winger down the outside.'

There might be one or two things that could be changed at half-time, but basically it was, 'Be patient. It might take you fifty minutes, it might take you sixty, it might take you seventy, it might take you less. It might take you eighty minutes to win it, but don't get frustrated, because ninety minutes is a long time.'

One season we scored goals in the last five minutes of about nine matches and this gave us another psychological lever. I told our players, 'As time wears on they are becoming more afraid of you. When their trainer says there are only ten minutes to go, that makes them all the more jittery. "Christ, they are due one now", they think.'

Many times near the end of matches I would say to the chairman, 'We'll get a bloody goal. They're wilting now and they are afraid.' With our team crossing the ball so much they would be getting a bit fidgety, and all of a sudden – boof! We had scored another goal. I remember the last kick of a game against Norwich. Phil Boersma retrieved the ball on the byline and Kevin Keegan came and boomeranged it into the net. What a heartbreak!

We got to the point where we knew we would win, just as we did with our first great team. We would have been playing for only ten minutes when I would know we were going to win. I have seen a team score against us and then change the whole pattern of their game. They started defending their 1–0 lead after ten minutes. Now that is defeatism. They should have gone on the way they were playing. If it is good enough to get a goal, it is good enough to stick with. But I have seen this repeatedly. I have seen it happen many times in matches in which Liverpool have not been involved.

The season we won the League and the UEFA Cup we played about eight League cup-ties on top of everything else, so we had a really heavy programme. And when we played the Germans, Borussia Mönchengladbach, they were the best team in Europe, with players like Netzer, Vogts, Danner, Wimmer, Heynckes, Bonhof and Jensen.

It was a two-legged final, and our big break came in the first game at Anfield. John Toshack didn't play that night. Brian Hall was in the team. It was pouring with rain and the ground was flooded. After half an hour with no goals, the referee, an Austrian, stopped the game and took the players off.

I had been down to see him and he had said, 'If it doesn't get any better, we will have to stop it because the ball won't shift. It won't move.'

I said, 'It's not too bad' – because I knew these Continentals. If I had said , 'Oh, yes, put it off,' he might have thought, 'Oh, oh – he *wants* it off.' So I said, 'It's not too bad, really. I've seen worse grounds than that.'

He said, 'No. I was on it. I know. I'll go out and try to kick the ball on it.'

So he went out and when he came back he said, 'No, the game is off until tomorrow.'

Boy, was I glad to hear that! I said to big John Toshack. 'Get away home to your bed, son, and get a rest for God's sake – you are playing tomorrow night.'

We'd seen something during that half an hour's play in the rain – something that was to win us the Cup. The German defenders weren't very big and they never came out of the penalty box. When English teams win the ball, they run out and you have to be quick to get moving. The Germans didn't. They stayed in. They didn't bother rushing out, and none of them was brilliant in the air. Actually, I was a little bit annoyed with the men who had vetted the team for us.

The game went on again the following night – we let spectators into the ground for a small price – and John Toshack played. From the start we were pumping the ball into the middle and John was flicking it on with his head. Kevin Keegan scored a couple of goals from these flicks and we won 3–0.

So we went to Mönchengladbach for the return game. They had a compact little stadium and the grass was brilliant. It was so dry that at first I thought it was artificial, made from nylon or something. About half an hour before the game a terrible storm came on: thunder and lightning and rain. The rain put more pace into the pitch and, boy, did the Germans give us a going-over for twenty minutes! I thought, 'Oh, dear God, we'll get beaten 15–0 here.' The way they were playing was untrue, but they had spent themselves a quarter of an hour before half-time. I could see right away that they had gone, that they had taken it all out of themselves. I said, 'We'll win the tie and we might even win this match.' They had gone – but so had we. We had played so many games that season – twice as many as Mönchengladbach – and if it hadn't been for end-of-season fatigue, I believe we would have scored a couple of goals in the second half. On the night, the Germans were the better team, and won 2–0, but we beat them 3–2 on aggregate.

A few minutes from the final whistle I got up and started to walk along the touchline. A German supporter was shouting at me and I said, 'Listen, you . . .' I was all right, because there was a wire fence between us, so he couldn't get near me. As I walked I talked to our players, saying, 'It's all right boys, it's all over.' I remember Big John Toshack was too shattered to be elated. It wasn't just the game that had tired him out, it was the whole season of games he had played for us and games he had played for Wales.

So we had won the League championship and we had won a cup in Europe, which was a double nobody else had done. We had achieved this with virtually a team of kids, so they were on their way then.

The following season, 1973–74, we were runners-up in the League and went to Wembley for the FA Cup. We had one shake on the way, when we drew at home with Doncaster Rovers. We usually did something like that in the Cup. When we won it in 1965, Stockport held us to a draw at Anfield.

I didn't see that game. I was away watching Bremen play Cologne, our opponents in the European Cup. It was the first Liverpool game I had missed. I thought we had a good chance, playing Stockport County at home. The game in Bremen was played in the afternoon, so I caught the Continental express train to Hamburg and a plane to London. A pal of Willie Stevenson's, who played for Rangers at one time, was at the passport office at London airport and I asked him, 'Are there any shock results?'

'Yes,' he said. 'Peterborough have beaten Arsenal at Peterborough.'

I said, 'Well, that's not really a big shock. Give me a look at your paper.'

I looked and I said, 'Liverpool one, Stockport one – is that not a surprise to you?'

When I got back to Liverpool, Bob Paisley told me the ground had been treacherous. It had frozen and then gone soft, so any result was possible. Bob said, 'I'll tell you candidly, we were lucky to get a draw.'

Against Doncaster we were 2–1 down with twenty-five minutes to go and Kevin Keegan, who comes from Doncaster, scored to make it a draw. I said to Kevin after the game, 'It is probably the most important goal you have scored up to the present, son, and maybe the most important one you'll ever score, because not only will it give the people of Doncaster a chance to see you play, but it might also win us the Cup.' They did see him play, and we did win the Cup.

We made a change that season. Larry Lloyd, who had been a very sound player for us at the heart of the defence, had a damaged leg muscle, and we brought in young Phil Thompson, who was promising to become a great player. A lot of players promised to be great of course, but I was sure about Phil. While he didn't have the frame of a lion, he did have the heart of a lion. So Phil and Emlyn filled the centre back positions and, whilst they weren't as rugged as Larry, we could alter our style of play. And we had Peter Cormack, signed from Nottingham Forest for £110,000 in 1972. Peter was playing very well, so we started poking the ball about from defence.

I am sometimes asked how much debate goes into the signing of a player. Often, for a big club like Liverpool, the answer is simple : if a player of good calibre becomes available you have got to be in the market, because they don't come very often.

In the case of Peter Cormack, the boy was at loggerheads with his club, Nottingham Forest. Though I had seen Peter play, my brother Bob in Scotland knew him, so I contacted Bob and we talked about him. Bob told me Peter could play up front, could play in the middle of the field and could also play wing half. Bob said Peter was brilliant in the air and gutsy. I did this home-work before Peter became available, and when he was put up for sale I knew he was the player for us. I bought him as a utility player, because he could play with either a number eleven or a number four on his back.

On two occasions I was unable to sign players I wanted because they failed our medical examinations. The first was in 1964, when Freddie Hill was the best player in England. I once saw Freddie when he was twenty-three, playing inside forward for Bolton against West Ham on a Saturday night. West Ham were a useful side, and Liverpool were due to play them in a cup-tie. Freddie tore them to pieces. In fact someone said to me, 'How do you beat West Ham?' and I said, 'Buy Freddie Hill!'

We agreed terms with Bolton and were ready to pay £45,000 for Freddie. He came over to Anfield one Monday lunchtime and I said, 'Have you trained, Freddie?' He said he had, so I said, 'Well, we'll go down to the doctor now.' The doctor ex-amined Freddie and said, 'Blood pressure.' So that was that. I said, 'The doctor's turned you down, Freddie.' Bill Ridding, the Bolton manager, was with us and said, 'Oh, he's fit.' So we went to see another doctor for a second opinion and he told us the same thing. That was enough for me. Bolton then took Freddie to a specialist, who said the boy was fit, and he played against us at Anfield two weeks later, on a Friday night before the Grand National.

Freddie's career continued of course. In fact Malcolm Allison took him to Manchester City and said he would make him the fittest player in the whole world. But the point was he was not fit enough to sign for Liverpool.

About eight years later the same thing happened in the case of Frank Worthington, the big Huddersfield Town forward. I visualized Worthington causing no end of trouble to opposing defences. I was ready to pay £150,000 for him. But again the doctor diagnosed blood pressure. We sent Frank on holiday to see if he just needed a rest, but when he came back his blood pressure was worse. So we did not go through with the deal.

I didn't turn down Freddie Hill and Frank Worthington. The medical profession turned them down. The fact that I was willing to buy them says enough about their ability. But if the specialist says, 'No, you shouldn't sign him,' then you've got to listen. If a player is fundamentally fit, we can make him fitter. But first we need the go-ahead from the doctor.

Leicester City bought Frank for £110,000 and he went on to play for England. I am delighted for him. As with Freddie Hill, Frank's ability was never in doubt. But neither player had the necessary qualifications, physically, to sign for Liverpool.

Lou Macari had every qualification to join Liverpool and I tried to sign him before he went to Manchester United. I saw Lou play for Celtic and I saw him play for Scotland and I had no doubt that he was the player for us. I saw Lou as a front man or a middle man – as a man who could play anywhere. Lou is small, but he is useful in the air, can tackle, plays with determination, and – most important – he is a brainy player.

I was willing to pay £200,000 for Lou. He came to watch one of our games and afterwards we discussed a possible transfer. Manchester United were also interested in signing him and he said he wanted time to think things over. In the end, Lou chose to go to United. He joined a team that was struggling and was on its way down to the Second Division.

If he had come to Liverpool he would not have had a lean spell. He would have settled in alongside players like Kevin Keegan. But the decision was his, and I have admired the way he has come through with United. He had a dog's life playing up front for a while, but he stuck to the job and is now magnificent in the middle of Tommy Docherty's young team. Lou can visualize the whole of the play and makes the other players think.

Another player who has changed his position is Ray Kennedy, the last man I bought for Liverpool and my most expensive signing at £200,000. Negotiations with Arsenal for Ray went on for months and I had left the club before he actually started playing in the team.

Ray had his problems, but he had ability and was still short of being twenty-three when we signed him. He had worked tremendously hard for Arsenal and was perhaps a little tired and in need of a change. I saw Ray as a man who could shoot with power and accuracy and I think he could have continued to play at the front if he had persevered. But Liverpool now play him in the middle and he has shown a lot of ability. His final pass is a dangerous one and he can still move up into good scoring positions.

Kennedy was the last player I signed, and it looks as if the transfer market will soon see some big changes with the introduction of greater freedom of movement for the players in what is called 'freedom of contract'. This will give players the freedom to move from one club to another as soon as their contract expires. The player will negotiate his own fee and the clubs will then agree upon a compensation figure based on the age and ability of the player.

All this is happening at a time when the country is in a poor financial state, with devaluation and unemployment. The football clubs that were struggling before are likely to face an even greater struggle. Whatever else happens when players get greater freedom of movement, it seems certain that the big will get bigger and the small will get smaller.

We beat Newcastle at Wembley in 1974 – but I think we won the Cup at Newcastle. We went there and used the whole width of St James's Park, which isn't the best of playing pitches, incidentally, and where there is always a wind blowing around the top of the hill. It is not the best of pitches, but it is a big pitch. So we started poking the ball around St James's. Alan Waddle played centre forward for us that day and we created seven chances. We didn't score any – Alan might have had three or four and was unlucky not to get one of them, and McFaul made brilliant saves at the feet of people – but we had played the way the Continental teams had played. We had used the width of the pitch, held on to the ball and made long, stringing passing movements; five or six passes from man to man. But there were no goals and the majority of the press boys were saying the game had been dull, so I came out and said to the gathering, 'That's the way to play – apart from scoring goals. And Alan Waddle, who is inexperienced, might have got three or four. We didn't give Newcastle a kick of the ball on their own pitch, which wasn't fair, because it was their ball!'

Our performance at Wembley was equivalent to the one at Newcastle apart from the fact that at Wembley the surface was better and we put three goals in the back of the net. If we had put three in the back of the net at Newcastle, the press would have gone raving mad about the game. They would have written, 'This is brilliant stuff. This is the way to play.'

On match day the BBC linked me up with Joe Harvey for a talk on television from our hotels. When Joe and I had finished our *tête à tête* and I was taking off the microphone harness, I said, 'Jesus Christ, Joe Harvey is beaten already and the bloody game hasn't even started.' I heard David Coleman laughing and I realized what I had said had gone over. I hadn't meant it to, because we had finished our talk. Joe and I sat together at Wembley, which was an unusual thing for rival managers to do. But that's the way we felt about it. We had known each other for a long time.

For me, that game was the culmination of things. The ground was suitable for play and we won 3–0. In one move we strung together twelve passes and on the thirteenth the ball was put into the net by Kevin Keegan.

When it was all over, the hullabaloo started and I said to the players, 'Go up to the Newcastle end. They are great supporters, just like your own.' And they went up and were given a big ovation. A couple of boys from Liverpool were down on their knees, kissing my feet. 'Make a good job of the boots, will you?' I said, just as a laugh, because they were good boys. In actual fact those boys have been to my house. Some people scoffed at the boys down on their knees, but they shouldn't have scoffed at that at all. I didn't gloat over it. Oh, no, it was respect for me. Yes. And it was respect for Liverpool, for the way the team had played. It was respect for everybody really. They weren't kneeling down to me because I was God or anything. They were pleased that they had won something. They were proud. I'm not interested in the people who scoff at things like that. I scoff at the scoffers.

It's the same with the controversy about players kissing each other when they score a goal. That's not being effeminate. It's not kissing really. These are hard boys, able to fight at the drop of a hankie, and, whilst I don't like to see the kissing, who can avoid it? It's all about fervour and pride. The players are involved. They are fighting for the supporters. If they have scored a goal in an important match, who is going to stop them from hugging each other? The people who scoff haven't been in that position. They don't know the feeling.

The season before the Cup Final, when we had won the League, I had been over to the Kop at Anfield and was on my way back when a policeman took hold of a red scarf as if it was a ragamuffin's. I told him off. 'Don't you do that,' I said. 'That's precious.' Those kind of things annoy me.

We had won the Cup and had given an exhibition of football the way it should be played. I handed my raincoat to a BBC producer. 'You carry that,' I said. 'Look after it. If you don't, you will have to pay for it, and I got it in Rotterdam, and the fare to Rotterdam is very expensive. Christ, you will be proud to carry Bill Shankly's coat down to the dressing-room. I'll get you in the programme next season if you make a good job of it.'

I didn't go up to the Newcastle end. I should have done really, because they are wonderful people and when I go to Tyneside the crowd is good to me and I always have banter with the people in the paddock. The crowds were good to me of course. I never got jeers.

When I go back to all these places, to the grounds where I've been as a player and a manager, I get a wonderful reception. The hospitality of the clubs has been brilliant – probably because they are saying, 'I'm glad that bugger is not here on business!'

13 Goodbye Anfield

After the FA Cup Final I went into the dressing-room – the BBC man had taken in my coat of course! – and I felt tired from all the years. I said to a bloke who was looking after the dressing-room, 'Get me a cup of tea and a couple of pies, for Christ's sake.'

When I sat down with my tea and my pies, my mind was made up. If we had lost the Final I would have carried on, but I thought, 'Well, we've won the Cup now and maybe it's a good time to go.' I knew I was going to finish.

We had played so well we could have won by a cricket score. We had achieved this performance in the showplace of football in this country and we knew where the team was going. It was known then that the Charity Shield game would be played at Wembley and I thought I would be back for that – though I might not be the manager.

When we had beaten Newcastle, and the players had put on their clothes, everything simmered down a little bit. Everybody was satisfied then, and we had the Cup ready to take on to the bus. I said to myself, 'That's it.'

Kevin Keegan sensed my feelings then. He said so later. I didn't go running around celebrating with the team. I didn't get carried around. I let the players have the arena. I was satisfied and I was tired.

A series of things went into my decision. I had been in the game for more than forty years, as a player and as a manager, and it had been hard work. I had been to outposts like Carlisle, Grimsby, Workington and Huddersfield, where there had been a lot of good players but no real ambition. When you have to sell players it is difficult to have success.

Then I had been at Liverpool, where I thought I had achieved most of the things I wanted to achieve. I would like to have won the European Cup, of course, but I had won most other things. I had been around a long time and I thought I would like to have a rest, spend more time with my family and maybe get a bit more fun out of life. Whilst you love football, it is a hard, relentless task which goes on and on like a river. There is no time for stopping and resting. So I had to say I was retiring. That's the only word for it, though I believe you retire when you are in your coffin and the lid is nailed down and your name is on it.

Deep down I had thought about it the previous season. Ness had said, 'How long is this going to go on?' I had said, 'I can't tell you.' That wasn't even Nessie's business. It was mine and mine alone.

When I talked to her about it later, she said, 'Are you sure you want to do that?' She didn't want me to do anything that I didn't want to do – and this didn't help me. I suppose I wanted her to say, 'Now is the time.' But we had just won the Cup and had been second in the League and the future was glowing, because Liverpool had built up a system. People respected them so much it bordered on fear.

I had been at Liverpool for fifteen years, and in a sense we had raised them from the dead. It was a terrible wrench to say, 'I'm going,' because after we had won the Cup in 1974 one of the thoughts that crossed my mind was, 'If I stay next season we will win the League, so that would be two teams of mine that won the League, the Cup and the League again in three seasons.' At the Cup Final dinner I said, 'The League is only a formality next season. This team is ready for anything.'

The boys were the right age, not too old and not too young. When a season starts, most of the teams say, 'If we get thirty-six points, we'll be all right,' but I used to say, 'If we get thirty-six points by Christmas, we will be all right.' I was so confident that

Liverpool would win the League again that I backed them heavily, with a saver on Derby.

If Don Revie had packed in at Leeds earlier I might have said, 'Oh, it might be easier now. I'd better stay on!' Leeds were going to be unsettled for a little while, because new men were coming in and the apple-cart was upset. That was the time to grab the lead again, quickly. I could have waited until the smoke cleared at Leeds. And if Don had joined Everton, as he might have done at one stage, I would have stayed at Liverpool to fight him!

All things being equal, and having been in the game a long time, I might have been better saying, 'Look, I'm going to have three or four months off, then I'll start all over again.' But I didn't. I thought that would have been unfair to the club. That would just have been using them.

Making the decision final was like being on a jury and having to say, 'Right, we'll hang him.' It took a time for me to come out and say, 'I'll go now,' but I felt the club was in a good position financially, had trophies in the cupboard and had a good team. If you leave a club when it is on the slide, people will point at you. On the other hand, they may say, 'He left when they were at the top – maybe he's frightened they are going to slide.' That was definitely wrong because I said I was willing to give the club all the co-operation I could. If they had been struggling, I wouldn't have gone.

Nobody made me pack in. It was worked out by myself and Ness. John Smith, who had been the chairman for a year, offered me another contract. In fact he kept reminding me about it. He said, 'Are you worrying about the contract? How long do you want it?' I could have stayed on with an increased salary.

Weeks and weeks went by and I was not enjoying life at all until I could get it sorted out. I then suggested to the directors that the only way to make the changeover was to promote the rest of the staff.

Most of those men had been at Anfield longer than I had and had picked up the system just like taking their tea. The system was practical and simple and Anfield was a bastion. They were sensible and sound men. I had elevated them earlier with a view to what I was going to do later on. Bob Paisley, who was number two to me, had worked hard and long for Liverpool, and I felt he should become the manager.

Joe Fagan was the first-team trainer and Ronnie Moran had taken charge of the reserves. We had brought in Roy Evans and had made him a trainer when he was only twenty-seven. Reuben Bennett was watching rival teams for us. Reuben is a tremendous man, and he had travelled with me more than anybody else on the staff. And Tom Saunders was looking after the youth development. Tom had been a schoolmaster and had been in charge of the Liverpool boys team. His work at Anfield produced players like Jimmy Case and David Fairclough.

I knew that if somebody was brought in from outside it would disrupt the place. This has happened at many places. It can be like throwing a cat in amongst the hens – the hens will fly over the bloody top. Not only that, but the men who had done so well for the club would have said, 'What are we working for? Christ, there's a vacancy, and in comes somebody else!' They might even have got humped out by a new man. So I put my reasons for wanting the staff to remain the same to the directors, because I felt it was fair and also necessary. And that is what happened.

I retired as manager of Liverpool, but that didn't mean I had retired from the world. Oh, no!

There is no respite for a football manager. Even through the summer, and when he is on holiday, he is still bubbling. It is difficult to relax, no matter how tough and strong he is. I wasn't feeling ill or anything like that, but I thought that if I was away from the pressures of Anfield for a while, and rested, it would make me fitter and rejuvenate me. I felt I could contribute more later on. I would never leave the city of Liverpool, and I still wanted to be involved in football. I still wanted to help Liverpool, because the club had become my life. But I wasn't given the chance.

I have a pension scheme and I had a testimonial, which was marvellous, an unforgettable evening, but I was willing to work for the club for nothing more than my pension. I was willing to help in any capacity, just to advise, if necessary, so that there would be no disruption at all while Bob got run-in.

Everything would have been clear with the club. I would have taken my cards. But I would have been in touch, and if anybody had had any problems, I could have helped. Maybe the problems didn't crop up. Maybe they didn't need my advice.

I went to the training ground at Melwood for a while. It is only down the road from where I live. But then I got the impression that it would perhaps be better if I stopped going. I felt there was some resentment – 'What the hell is he doing here?' So I changed my life. I still do a bit of training to keep myself in reasonable shape and to have something to do which resembles what I used to do, and there are plenty of other places to train where I am welcomed. I packed up going to Melwood and I also stopped going into the directors' box at Anfield. I still go to matches, of course. I sit in the stand. I would have loved to have been invited to away matches, but I waited and waited until I became tired of waiting.

Finally, after twenty months and after Liverpool had won the League championship again, I was invited to travel with the club to Bruges for the second leg of the UEFA Cup Final. I accepted, because I didn't want anybody to think I was petty, but it came too late for my peace of mind. I couldn't help wondering why it had taken them so long. And I was not impressed with the arrangements they made for me in Bruges, where I was put into a different hotel to the one used by the official party. I found that quite insulting.

The invitation to Bruges could not make up for the previous twenty months, when it would have been the greatest thing in the world for me if Liverpool had been playing at Middlesbrough or Tottenham, and had said, 'Would you like to go?' I would have said, 'Oh, yes, certainly I would like to go.' Some of the directors invite their friends to the games. I wouldn't have been in the way. I wouldn't have done any harm. But I would have been associated in some way, and amongst them, and I would have been just as anxious as the manager of the team for them to win, because they were all my players.

I soon realized that Liverpool preferred me to make my own arrangements, so that's what I started to do. I asked other clubs for tickets, sometimes when Liverpool were the visiting team and sometimes to see other teams play. And I have not been short of invitations from other clubs, either. Derby County invited me to a match, and West Ham asked me to be their guest when they played Liverpool in the FA Cup. Ron Greenwood, West Ham's general manager, couldn't have been nicer. We even had a meal together. Tommy Docherty invited me to Old Trafford when Manchester United played Liverpool in a night match. Tommy invited me to have a meal with him in the restaurant at Old Trafford and we enjoyed a wonderful hour of banter before the match.

Sidney Reakes, the Liverpool director, said to Tommy, 'I see Bill Shankly's here.'

'Aye,' said Tommy. 'He's welcome here.'

I might add that I count Everton amongst the clubs who have welcomed me over the last few seasons. I have been received more warmly by Everton than I have been by Liverpool.

It is scandalous and outrageous that I should have to write these things about the club I helped to build into what it is today, because if the situation had been reversed I would have invited people to games. It would have been a wonderful honour to have been made a director of Liverpool Football Club, but I don't go round saying, 'I would like to be this and that.' That's begging – and I'm not a beggar! No, no – anything I have done and everything I have got, I have worked for.

It was never my intention to have a complete break with Liverpool, but at the same time I wasn't going to put my nose in where it wasn't wanted. Maybe I was an embarrassment to some people. Maybe they thought I should have asked them if I wanted to go to away matches. Maybe they didn't even think about it. That's their business, nothing to do with me.

Whatever happens now, I shall always think back with special happiness to one particular period of my time at Anfield which represented everything I could have hoped for in the organization and running of a football club. That was when Eric Roberts was the chairman, Eric Sawyer the financial director and Peter

Robinson the secretary. We had a wonderful working relationship. Funnily enough, I met the Liverpool representatives at the home of Mr Roberts's father, Robson Roberts, who was a director when I was interviewed for the job.

I have worked for a lot of football directors and I have known many others. In the main, directors are genuine fellows, and it is not an easy job. They have to be discreet and they have to know what they are talking about. They have to have a knowledge of business and they have to have a knowledge of the game. They are men of influence in the making of a successful football club. You need good players, a good training staff – all in tune with the manager – good directors and a good secretary.

When I came to Liverpool the secretary was Jimmy McInnes, who died. Jimmy was honest and he was also quick-tempered. Sometimes he could be rude to people – some of them needed it, and he was right – but he would be gentlemanly with people he respected. There were some of us at Anfield with whom he never had a harsh word. Others would find him difficult to deal with and hard to understand. I've heard him calling somebody on the telephone and suddenly, bang! The phone would go down.

Jimmy loved a game of snooker, and he was a good player. It was a change from his chores as secretary. When the club began to be transformed, Jimmy got the lash of the success. There were only a few seats in the stand in those days and when we won the Second Division championship, reached the FA Cup semi-final, won the First Division championship and then won the Cup, Jimmy's work was doubled and everything began to pile up on top of him. He needed help. He needed to be able to delegate some of the work.

That is when Peter Robinson came in. He had gained experience in the lower divisions and was at Brighton when their manager, Archie Macaulay, phoned me one day to recommend him, and I told the board. I don't know whether that was the reason Peter got the job, but I certainly put his name forward. Peter came, and has been a huge success.

Above all, Peter knows people and how to deal with them. He knew me. I didn't try to tell Peter anything about his job, and he didn't try to tell me anything about mine. And he came along at the right time, when the club was becoming more and more successful and the ground was about to be rebuilt.

For about three years, our foursome – Mr Roberts, Mr Sawyer, Peter and I – settled anything at the club that needed to be settled, and during that period, the team won the League championship and the UEFA Cup in the same season. I am not suggesting just the four of us won the double for the club, but everything ran smoothly, everything was right – the board of directors, the staff and the team.

I could never be fully involved in the running of a club again, even though I have not been short of offers, but I thought I might have been invited to have helped my country in some way since I left Liverpool Football Club. I am not suggesting that I should have been appointed manager of Scotland. Indeed not. But I feel sure I could have given Scotland some assistance. I have often felt that Scotland have not been able to get the best out of the talented players they have had, and at times it has been painful to sit and watch the Scottish team under the hammer, as when they were beaten 5–1 by England at Wembley in 1975.

I proved myself as a player and I proved myself with my record as a club manager. Perhaps some people see me as the domineering type who takes everything over. That is a myth. I am ambitious not only for myself but for everyone I work for and work with. The footballers of my country have always had so much potential and so much passion for the game, and I am certain I could have brought out even more of the Bruce and Wallace in them.

What I have in mind now is helping people in the game in some way or other. I could be watching players, or teams; giving advice, seeing that the training was right, passing on what it has taken me all the years to learn. Nothing is new, of course. We had tactical talks at Preston for two and a half hours – half an hour about a goal we had lost. The goalkeeper had started it – and in the end he blamed the outside left !

14 The Managers

Bob Paisley took on a big job when he became manager of Liverpool, but I felt he had the necessary qualities to be capable of doing it. You can't show greater faith in a man than to recommend him to be your successor.

Bob and I had worked together from the first day I walked into Anfield, and we had learned from each other. Bob is quiet and might be a little more withdrawn than I am, but he is knowledgeable. He knows all about the training of players and how to deal with them psychologically.

Perhaps some of my psychology has rubbed off on Bob. I'm not saying that he copies me, but he might say to himself, 'Well, I remember one time such-and-such happened and Bill did that I'll do the same.' On the other hand, he might say, 'Oh, I'll do it differently. I'll do it my way.'

In the 1975–76 season, Bob took Liverpool to a record ninth League championship, which was a magnificent achievement. It had been one of my ambitions to win that ninth championship and, if I couldn't win it myself, I wanted the club to win it. It meant that Liverpool were the champions of champions, even though other clubs had spent more time in the First Division.

The same season, Liverpool repeated the 1972–73 League Championship and the UEFA Cup double, beating Bruges in the final 4–3 on aggregate (3–2 at home and 1–1 away) and Bob earned another of my old titles, manager of the year. Bob and I

– and the rest of the staff at Liverpool – battled for fifteen years against the fiercest competition imaginable, and the League positions show that during that period, no club in England was more consistent than ours.

A couple of years after I came to Liverpool, Harry Catterick became the manager of Everton. When Harry had finished at Sheffield Wednesday, I phoned him to say I was sorry to hear about it, and when I got the job at Anfield he wrote to me, wishing me the best of luck. I also sent him a wire wishing him all the best for his first League game as manager of Everton.

Harry's nature is to be withdrawn and cagey. He was just as intense as me and was hell-bent on winning, but he did things in a different way. Possibly he tried to do things in a more diplomatic way. I used to call him 'Happy Harry' and he called me 'Rob Roy', but deep down we were very friendly – we spoke to each other once a year!

Let's not be hypocritical. You need friendship in football, but only to a certain extent. I mean, I wasn't concerned who beat Everton. We respected each other and we'd be happy to be first and second in the League – the other fellow second of course. One season we won the League and Everton won the FA Cup. Everybody was happy then. But only winning is success. I remember seeing an American gangster film, and one of the characters said, 'Foist is foist and second is nut'n.' Then he took his gun and shot a bloke. Not many can be first in football.

In 1961–62 Liverpool won the Second Division championship. In 1962–63 Everton won the First Division championship. In 1963–64 Liverpool won the First Division championship. In 1964–65 Liverpool won the FA Cup. In 1965–66 Liverpool won the First Division championship and Everton won the FA Cup. In 1969–70 Harry won his second League championship, and in 1972–73 (Harry stepped down as Everton's manager in the April of 1973) Liverpool won the League title.

You couldn't get a ticket for the Mersey Derby games for love nor money. The grounds were packed to capacity and the rivalry was unbelievable. There was no enjoyment for managers the whole week before a Derby game, and the matches were usually dull, because nobody wanted to lose. If you lost, you felt terrible. You felt as if you had let the people down. The feeling was not for yourself, but for the people who supported you. They were in the same city. If they supported the team that had lost, they got pestered to death when they went back to work on Monday. It soon wore off of course. Like today's news, next week it's forgotten.

In 1967 we were beaten 1–0 by Everton at Goodison Park in the fifth round of the FA Cup. The game was televised on to a screen at Anfield, so sixty thousand people watched the game at Goodison and forty thousand saw it on the screen at Anfield. We also met Everton in the FA Cup semi-final at Old Trafford in 1971, and that was a very good match. They had a good first half and we played well in the second half and won 2–1.

One day Everton came to Anfield when half their first-team regulars, including Alex Young, were out with injuries – and they beat us 4–0. I said, 'Harry, I wish to Christ you had been at full strength!' The reversal of that was in 1966, when we won the championship – and we weren't half some team! We beat Everton 5–0 at Anfield. 'Listen, Harry,' I said. 'We should have won 6–0 at Tottenham last week. We gave them the drubbing of their lives. So this was coming to somebody.' We were winning 5–0 and we were like vultures, still looking for goals. No slacking off.

Johnny Morrissey was the last player to be transferred between the two clubs in my time. He went from Liverpool to Everton. It causes a bit of argument when a player goes from one local club to another, but it shouldn't make any difference really. We tried to get David Johnson from Everton, but in the end he went to Ipswich. We had great players and Everton had great players. Bobby Collins knew the game and was strong : a good competitor. Alan Ball is another competitor – one of the greatest players in England since the war.

I went to see Harry when he was ill. When people are sick all the rivalry goes and the barriers come down. Harry is a shrewd businessman and a good manager. He had successes enough at Everton, and he took Sheffield Wednesday out of the Second

Division and got them to second place in the First. His record speaks for itself.

Harry had the backing of John Moores, a director who knows the game from A to Z, has shrewd judgement when it comes to assessing players and always talks sense. The combination of Harry and Mr Moores was formidable, but opposition can be a good thing. They made me fight even harder.

Billy Bingham was manager of Everton in opposition to me for a short period, and during that time we became good friends. Billy had a difficult task trying to keep up with Liverpool.

My rivalry with Don Revie was a little bit different, because we were further apart geographically. The rivalry between Liverpool and Leeds has been one of the greatest in the history of English football, if not the greatest.

Don is different from Harry in many ways, but there was a similarity in their quietness and in the way they went about things. Don is obviously an efficient man. I was at Huddersfield when he went to Leeds and the Leeds United ground was an awful place. He built the club up, so that they had a wonderful ground, with a lot of seats. The playing pitch was one of the worst in England but now it is one of the best.

He is the type who likes to hear others do the talking, but he was always open enough with me. I gave him a laugh. He seemed to be a fellow who was short of laughs, and when he was with me he laughed so hard that I thought, 'Well, he hasn't had a laugh for two months!'

Don is a very superstitious man, which I felt was a weakness. He would always wear the same suit and when the whistle blew for the captains to toss up, Billy Bremner used to come to the side of the pitch and give Don a ring off his finger, and Don would put it in his pocket. I always felt that being as superstitious as that could be a bad thing. If Billy's ring had been lost, for instance – which could have been arranged! – he might have been depressed and thought, 'Christ, we'll lose today!'

We discussed the game together many times, and possibly Don gave his opinions to me more than anybody else. These conversations helped us both, because we talked about details and how to

deal with players. I knew Don's approach. Perhaps I was th
only one who did know it. You could say we were as thick a
thieves.

The Liverpool–Leeds matches took over from the local Derbie
in a sense. For six successive matches the gates were closed lon,
before the games started, home and away. My last two game
against Leeds at Anfield were amazing. We came out of our hide
out and couldn't even get to our own ground! The gates wer
closed and the ground was blocked off from about a quarter t
two. One time when we played at Leeds, Matt Busby didn'
manage to get to the game until half-time because of the crowd:

I don't see as much of Don now that he is manager of England
and I only hear from him occasionally. He has a harder job now
The worry is greater, because he has the nation on his back. H
is like the Prime Minister now. He is at war, and people don
want to lose a war.

He has a difficult job trying to deal with the different types c
players and their temperaments. At Leeds he lived with his playei
and knew them inside out. Now he has fellows that he knows bu
doesn't really know – not deep down. I don't envy him.

I have a feeling England will qualify for the World Cup fina
in Argentina, though the Italians will be very difficult to bea
They have ways and means of slowing the game down and thei
defensive set-up is useful. They are well-organized and can frust
rate you. Qualifying will be hard – and it will be even harder :
England get to Argentina. Of the sixteen teams left when the res
have been skimmed off, at least twelve will be able to play
Playing in Europe, where the climate can be similar to our owr
is one thing, but to go to Argentina, where the climate is differer
and where they tend to interpret the laws of the game differently
is something else. A terrible task.

Alf Ramsey won the World Cup. What more can you do tha:
that? I remember Alf as a player with Tottenham and as th
manager of Ipswich, before he took over England. He was
perfectionist, a stickler; dour and stubborn.

When I was the manager of Huddersfield we were drawn t
play Ipswich in an FA Cup-tie. There was a clash of colours, c

course, and I said to Alf, 'There's no good in both of us chang-ing. You play in your colours and we'll change.' The FA would accept that if it was mutually agreed between the clubs concerned.

'No,' said Alf. 'We have both got to change.'

I said, 'Well, we have got white jerseys and black pants and white stockings with an inch of blue band on them.' When the tops of the stockings were turned over, you couldn't see the blue band at all. But Ipswich also had blue in their stockings appar-ently.

'No, no,' said Alf.

I said, 'We'll borrow some red stockings.'

In the end he wrote to the FA, and we both had to change every stitch. I felt that was going a little bit too far. Maybe he wanted to do it right, to play to the rules. I don't know what his reasons were. Maybe he thought I was trying to get some kind of advantage over him. I suppose it was an example of the man's honesty. There was no deviousness about him at all.

At Ipswich, Alf had Jimmy Leadbeater, an outside left, playing very deep, and big Ted Phillips and Ray Crawford up the front. This took them out of the Second Division and won them the First Division championship, so possibly Alf could see that this would be successful at international level as well. But at inter-national level there must be wingers somewhere along the line.

Maybe Alf realized that losing is curtains in football and win-ning is everything. His plan was successful at Ipswich, and he introduced the same plan at international level – even though he had wingers. Peter Thompson was at his peak then, and Ian Callaghan could complement Peter on the other wing.

Alf played Peter a few times and then left him out, saying his final pass wasn't good enough and he didn't score enough goals. I agreed with him to a certain extent – but Alf didn't talk about the other things Peter did, grafting, turning the opposing team around and running them towards their own goal. Peter Thomp-son wasn't on the losing side very often at Liverpool. Perhaps when he played for England he didn't have the men alongside him who could read him well enough to take advantage of what he could do.

But Alf succeeded at Ipswich, which was the backwoods as far as football was concerned, and he won the World Cup. You can't argue against that. He had his own ways, which didn't suit everybody, but he had principles, not only as a manager but also as a man. All in all, a decent chap.

There are men in Britain who have the qualities the game needs. Matt Busby, Jock Stein, Stan Cullis, Joe Mercer and Bill Nicholson are experienced, responsible people who know the game and talk sense. They should be given more authority – real authority – so that their knowledge can be used to the best advantage.

Matt went to Old Trafford when Manchester United had nothing. The place was a bomb-site and he built the best club ground in England – a place out on its own, housing the biggest crowds in the country.

United lost a ground during the war, but later Matt lost a team and almost lost his own life as well. He is very human, and some people may get the impression that because he is kind he is also soft. They should be careful, because Matt can bite as well.

I have known Matt for many years and have spent many happy times at Old Trafford watching players like Denis Law, George Best and Bobby Charlton. I remember being there one day with Liverpool, before United started building the new stand on the far side, with luxury boxes. I think the dream of building that stand was with Matt on that particular day, because he was acting as if he was thinking how much success was needed to pay for it. We sat together where Tommy Docherty sits now, and Matt was puffing away at cigarettes. I said, 'Matt, you look worried, and our team hasn't even broke sweat yet.'

He said, 'That's what's worrying me – that they might break sweat!'

'Listen, Matt,' I said, 'if I could get overcoats with numbers on, I'd put them on my players for the second half to keep them warm.'

After the match I said to Chris Lawler, 'Do you know who that was who darted past you with ten yards to spare? Not Charlton or Best – it was Pat Crerand!'

We didn't give much away to United, or anybody else, but Matt built his new stand eventually, and later became a club director. He still plays an important part in club affairs and is also involved in many other projects, both inside and outside football. For instance, he is a member of the Football League Management Committee.

Jock Stein has had the kind of set-backs that would deter most people. A leg injury finished his playing career. He had a heart attack, and survived that. Then, on his way home from holiday, with my brother Bob in his car, he was involved in a road accident which brought him close to death. Like Matt Busby, Jock almost lost his life.

I would describe Jock as the Robert Bruce of football. He has the blood of Bruce in his veins, and that makes him a real warrior. His managerial career is unparalleled in Britain. Some people may argue that the Scottish League is inferior to the English League in strength. Nevertheless Jock achieved that tremendous run of nine successive championships with Celtic – and Celtic were the first British club to win the European Cup. No disrepect to Manchester United, but Celtic won it on foreign soil.

When Celtic beat Inter-Milan in the final in Lisbon, I was the only manager of an English club there to see it. I went into the dressing-room after the match and Jock had just stepped out of the bath. He'd had a bath because he'd been sweating during the game – that match was the ultimate for Jock.

Jock knows how to treat people. All good managers know this. Jock and I have been in similar situations with players. There are some you don't have to say a word to and there are others whose backs you have to be on all the time. Some players may get the impression that they are being ignored, but they are wrong.

Like me, Jock knows everyone who works for his club. He treats people as human beings, but he also has a violent temper and can tear a strip off them if necessary. And sometimes it is necessary. We can both be impatient. Jock is always in a hurry to get out of the Celtic car park. Even if his car is in the corner of a wall, Jock thinks he should just be able to climb in and drive away. I've seen him twisting his steering-wheel and I've said,

'You're not trying to take it off, are you Jock? You won't manage that!' If he's hemmed in by other cars, he'll say, 'Who the hell put those bloody cars there?' He thinks he should be able to drive straight through the wall and into London Road.

When he has got it into his head that something needs doing, and he knows he is right – when the penny drops – he wants to go, there and then. No waiting. 'Where's the bloody taxi? It should be here now,' he'll say – even though he only phoned for it a minute ago. He thinks taxis should drop out of the sky for him – and I'm the same.

If we have to do something terribly important and we see people dawdling about nonchalantly, smoking their pipes, we'll say, 'Christ, look at him!' We get frustrated, and people may think, 'Oh, they are going mad. They are arguing the toss. They have lost their heads!' But that is wrong – very much wrong. We haven't lost our heads. We know what we are doing, within the frustration we feel.

I have seen managers sitting at games, puffing away at pipes or cigarettes and looking as cool as cucumbers – and inside they were bursting. I would be sitting and talking, saying things like 'Jesus, Christ, what's happening?' I'd be talking non-stop at times, giving vent to my feelings, letting out the steam so it wouldn't collect and blow me up.

The ones who sit quietly – 'Look how calm he is' – are often the ones who have heart attacks. There are other fellows who are naturally calm but who have no enthusiasm. What have you got without enthusiasm? The greatest gift in the world is ability, and after that you need natural enthusiasm to make the most of ability. I would tell those who don't have that to get the hell out of the game.

Stan Cullis was another manager who would make unbelievable noises while he was watching a match. He used to shout to players who were on the far side of the pitch. One day I remember him shouting 'Noddy!' at a player who was at the corner flag on the far side. Stan just kept shouting as if he could force his voice through a crowd of forty thousand people.

'He can't hear you, Stan,' I said.

Another night, at Blackpool, Wolves needed to win to clinch the League championship. Stan and a director were sitting in the stand and I'm sure they were trying to kick the ball out of the Wolves penalty box! Their legs were going, and Stan was shouting, 'No, No, don't do that!' Ronnie Flowers was pulling the ball down in the penalty box and giving passes, and Stan was shouting, 'No, Ron, no!' But in the end Ron was right. Wolves won.

During the game one of the Wolves players injured an eye, and Stan left his seat to see the boy. When he came back they were winning 1–0 with ten men. And he shouted and shouted. After the game, people might have thought Stan would be oblivious of what he had done and said – because as far as Stan was concerned, while the game was on he was on his own, nobody else existed – but they would have been wrong. Stan would be able to remember everything. He was in full control of himself really.

While Stan was volatile and outrageous in what he said, he never swore. And he could be as soft as mash. He would give you his last penny.

Stan was one-hundred-per-cent Wolverhampton. His blood must have been old gold. He would have died for Wolverhampton. He was one of the most successful men in the game, as a player – captain of Wolves at an early age – and as a manager. His record proves that, and on top of everything else, he laced a lot of European teams.

Above all, Stan is a clever man who could have been successful at anything. When he left Wolverhampton, I think his heart was broken and he thought the whole world had come down on top of him. But he recovered and became a managing director of companies.

He once defended a player for us at football's independent tribunal. Stan was with us as the representative of the Professional Footballers' Association, and he was brilliant – just like a lawyer. His description of the incident in question and the way he put points to the authorities and the referee and linesmen was magnificent.

All round, as a player, as a manager, and for general intelli
gence, it would be difficult to name anyone since the game begar
who could qualify to be in the same class as Stan Cullis.

Joe Mercer is another man who was a fantastic player and
manager, who won all the honours in the game, and has continued
to do a wonderful job for football. Things went wrong for him
at Aston Villa and Sheffield United. He had a bad start, but he
came back to win promotion and the League title, FA Cup
League Cup and European Cup-winners' Cup for Manchester
City, and now he is a director of Coventry City, Joe is a gentle
man, full of humour and steeped in the game. Joe is a real man

Bill Nicholson is a reserved type, but no soft mark. He brough
tremendous years of success to Tottenham and his teams played
great football. Bill can be dour. He doesn't often say much, bu
I always got on well with him, and I respect him.

You can't buy the kind of experience those men have.

Don Revie and I had a difficult time turning Leeds and Liver
pool into what they are today, but Brian Clough possibly had the
worst job of all at Derby County. He took them from nothing to
the championship of the First Division and built a world-class
team.

Cloughie did a hell of a job and I have a great deal of respect
for him. But I think he has said a lot of things he is sorry for. I'm
not suggesting what he said was not true, but sometimes it is better to keep the truth to yourself. He has offended people, and you
don't offend people in football if you can avoid it.

I didn't like the feud between Cloughie and Don Revie. It
would have been better if they hadn't gone on television together.
They were two sour men – but great managers – and it was an
unfortunate episode which both could have done without.

Derby now have another strong man at the helm in Dave
Mackay, a courageous player who has proved that he is also a
courageous manager. Dave has done wonderfully well considering
the trouble there was at the time he came. He pulled things together and enlarged upon what Cloughie had done by buying
great players that some people didn't fancy. He bought Francis
Lee from Manchester City and that move helped Derby win the

championship in 1975. He then took Charlie George from Arsenal, and the boy's attitude changed dramatically. Bruce Rioch has been a revelation since he joined Derby from Aston Villa. Mackay is the type of manager who is willing to back his assessment of players. He has a positive attitude, and that is why Derby will continue to have success even though other clubs have double the population and grounds twice the size. The Baseball Ground reminds me of the Leeds City Varieties Theatre – *The Good Old Days* on television. You feel that you can lean across the main stand and shake hands with the people on the far side of the ground.

For a small club, Derby think big, but if it hadn't been for Cloughie there would have been no need for Mackay or anybody else – because there would have been no Derby County as we know it today. Cloughie made Derby with his vital decisions and his vision of the game. He is young, so he could still become a force in the game again.

Tommy Docherty is another case in point. I thought Tommy was going to be unlucky all along the line. It was Tommy, of course, who took my place as a player at Preston. I cost £500 from Carlisle and Tommy cost £4000 from Celtic. He gave Preston ten full seasons of hard work, and ten Tommy Dochertys in a team would take some beating! But as a manager Tommy has had a varied career, to say the least.

He was unlucky at Chelsea, where he had some great players and a style of his own, quick control and passing movements, and his life as a manager continued to be up and down. Even when he became manager of Manchester United and managed to save a team that was on the slide from relegation, they went down the following season. But fate turned things the opposite way for Tommy and now the world is at his feet.

Like Derby, Manchester United have the foundations for success for years to come as long as they don't get blown away with their success. Sometimes Tommy's ego bursts and he blows his top, but he is a lot steadier now than he used to be. He works hard. He's at Old Trafford day and night. He lives and sleeps Manchester United. And he's sitting on a gold-mine.

There are times, in the heat of a match, when managers let their feelings get the better of them. I remember one occasion when Liverpool played a Second Division game at Bury, where Bob Stokoe was the coach at the time. That season Liverpool had beaten Bury 5–0 at Anfield, and they had lost one of their players with an injury in the first minute of that match. When we played at Bury the ground was packed and the whole of Liverpool seemed to be there. In the first minute, Gerry Byrne got in a hard tackle, and Bob, who was sitting fairly close to me, lost his temper.

'It's bloody happened again,' he said.

'It was an accident,' I said.

'No!' said Bob.

'Your man was a coward,' I told him. 'He was trying to jump away from Gerry when Gerry caught him. It's just a coincidence that you've got a player hurt again – the same as it's a coincidence that we're going to beat you again!'

'Go on, you so-and-so,' said Bob.

'Shut up,' I said.

'Do you want to fight or something?' said Bob.

'Let's go to the back of the stand – the quicker the better,' I said.

We were carrying on like a couple of children, but fortunately sanity prevailed. Liverpool were dominating the game and Liverpool supporters were dominating the terraces, so Bob may have felt that the whole world was fighting against him.

Since then Bob, a famous player with Newcastle United, has made a big name for himself as a manager. He went to Carlisle and saved my old club from extinction, he brought the FA Cup to Sunderland by beating Leeds United at Wembley, and then brought Sunderland back to the First Division.

Bob and I are very friendly. He's my type of man – he's a bad loser!

15 The Players

There have been players who have had a little publicity and have been naughty boys. They have done wrong, but I'm not sure that they were all basically wrong. I would have liked the chance to have used my psychology on some of them. I wouldn't guarantee that I could have done anything with them, but I had my way of dealing with players.

Take the case of Phil Boersma when he walked out on Liverpool at Wembley before the 1974 FA Cup Final. I gave the job of substitute that day to Chris Lawler, one of the greatest servants of all time, who was adaptable and could play in any of the centre-back positions if we had needed a little strength. Lawler could have gone in and Emlyn Hughes could have been thrown forward into the fray. Or we might have needed another defender for the last twenty minutes. That's why I did it. I wasn't trying to degrade Phil Boersma. Only one man could be substitute, and only one man made the decisions – and that was me. It took me until quarter to two on the day of the match to make that decision.

I didn't punish Boersma. He did what he thought was right. I said to him, 'Look, Phil, I'm sorry it happened, son, I'm sorry you did what you did, but you were listening to other people, not me. If you get your advice from sensible people, all right, I'll hold my hands up. But what you did was to insult Chris Lawler, not me. It was an insult to one of the finest boys ever to have played here. You should have gone up to him and said,

"Well done, Chris, I'm glad you are substitute, you've been a great player". But you didn't. I have nothing against you. As far as I'm concerned, it is finished.' And I didn't hold any grudges against him.

Now Phil has left Liverpool and has gone to Middlesbrough. So who was wrong and who was right? Phil Boersma, or Bill Shankly? I have nothing against Phil. He gave of his best when he played.

Tommy Smith also walked out on Liverpool one day. That was at Arsenal. But Tommy had a little more reason to do what he did than Phil had. Tommy had an idea he wouldn't be playing, and I wouldn't tell him. Tommy tried to badger me into telling him, but the more he badgered me the less chance he had of getting to know. I didn't tell Tommy anything until the time came, until I was ready. So Tommy walked out of Highbury. When Tommy used to shout the odds I would say, 'There's only one person you're frightening with that noise, and that's yourself – so bugger off and make a cup of tea for us!'

There was the incident involving Roger Hunt of course. When the substitution rule came, our policy was to pick our best team and only substitute a player if he was injured. Our plan of campaign was to keep playing on. It might not be right for seventy or eighty minutes, but we could win in the end. If a boy was playing really badly I'd say, 'If he's playing that bad, he must be ill, so we'd better bring him off in case he drops down dead!' Roger Hunt is a nice fellow and he possibly regretted what he did that night we played Leicester at Anfield in the FA Cup.

We were fighting a battle for our lives. We were a goal down and Roger wasn't playing well. On the bench we had Bobby Graham, a quick-fire player who might have broken through. We needed a little pace. I could have picked any one of the players to bring off, but I thought Roger was doing nothing by his standards. I sat for five or six minutes and thought, 'It's got to be Roger.' To take off Roger at Anfield was quite a difficult job, but I did it, and of course he threw off his jersey, which didn't help any.

Roger probably regretted that, because he did well for Liverpool and Liverpool did well for him. But I didn't say, 'He'll get fined,' or 'He'll get this, or that, or the other.' I said, 'I took Roger Hunt off. Nobody else but me. I take the blame for him. I'm responsible for the whole thing. What's more, if the same situation cropped up again and he was playing the same way as he was then, I would do the same again.'

I caused a hullabaloo. If we had been winning the match, nothing would have been said about it. But we were losing, and Roger knew he was having a lean time. He was one of the king-pins of Liverpool, make no mistake about that, but sometimes it is possible for a good player to play badly.

Kevin Keegan threw down his jersey at Wembley in the Charity Shield match, shortly after my retirement as manager of Liverpool. It was my farewell appearance with the team, and before the start I said to the man in charge of the band, 'Don't play now, because nobody will hear you – I'm going up to the Kop end!' It was that kind of occasion. It wasn't an FA Cup Final or a match for the League championship. The boys were playing for charity.

It was developing into an interesting game, but it was spoiled completely when Keegan and Billy Bremner were sent off. Leeds and Liverpool had been rivals for years and there had been no trouble. Then two players were sent off in the Charity Shield. It needn't have happened. Kevin Keegan was provoked. He took up an aggressive attitude, and next thing he was in a flare-up with Bremner. I didn't condone what they did, but the season hadn't bloody started!

The frustration of believing he had done nothing really wrong made Kevin take his jersey off. He must have thought to himself, 'Well, if I'm getting sent off for that, what the hell will they do if I really do something?' Kevin had just been in a little bit of trouble with England in Belgrade and was in a bit of turmoil at the time, but the boy did wrong to throw down his jersey. And Bremner did the same. I said to Billy after the game, in the Leeds team bus, 'What did you do that for? Why did you follow Kevin? You're thirty-one and he's twenty-three.' And he admitted I was right, that he was old enough to have known better.

I said to the referee, Bob Matthewson, 'You took something out of the charity box today, didn't you? You didn't put anything into it.'

So Kevin and Billy were suspended for three matches for being sent off and then they were called back for bringing the game into disrepute and were suspended again for a month and fined £500. I was astounded when I saw the verdicts. I would have been in fighting for Kevin from the first bell. I wouldn't have accepted it, and I'm not concerned what anybody else thinks. Kevin was a little bit aggressive that day, but he had been provoked. He had been knocked around. I felt that he was badly done by. So I would have been in fighting for him. Whether they would have kicked me out or not was another story, but I would have been in with my version of the whole thing.

The game was a showpiece at Wembley. If it had been a League match or even an FA Cup-tie, or if it had been played at Leeds or Liverpool or Old Trafford, I doubt whether they would have been sent off. Bob Matthewson is a good referee, one of the best in the game, because he knows the game. Perhaps he felt he had to send them off because of the occasion. All the football dignitaries were at the game, and there was the usual pomp of Wembley. I was annoyed about the whole business.

I didn't go into the dressing-room to see Kevin. I didn't want to upset him further with sympathy, because he didn't want sympathy. When you cut your finger it bleeds like hell, but a little later it stops bleeding. Kevin went home to Doncaster, and we went on to Glasgow for Billy McNeill's testimonial match. I had Maurice Setters' phone number in Doncaster and I contacted Maurice and asked him if he would go round to Kevin's home for us. Kevin came up and I said to him 'Everybody in Scotland has been waiting to see you. The Celtic supporters have been writing to me about it, son.' Kevin played, and it was an excellent match. I know Kevin. He's a good boy and is good to his family.

I met problem players – or so-called problem players – the whole of my time in football. But if the players had top-class ability as well as problems, I would have persevered with them.

Even if they had been in jail, I would have been waiting for them at the gate, saying, 'OK, boys, you've served your sentence, let's get started!'

George Best, Stan Bowles, Rodney Marsh and Charlie George all had reputations and Best is probably the classic case. He was one of the greatest players ever and even when he was very young he would have been recognized in Outer Mongolia. Every movement he made was seen and talked about and written about. In a sense, he was weak enough to fall for all this, and that made him a target for everybody. Every little mistake he made was pounced upon.

I would like to have tried to help him, but that wasn't my business. Possibly I would have tried to encourage him to bring over his family to Manchester. That might have made a difference. I don't know. I knew the boy, but only from a distance. You have got to live with people to see what they really are. But we had some famous players at Liverpool, and though there was the odd occasion when one stepped out of line, we didn't have the kind of trouble that Manchester United had with George.

On the night of Bobby Charlton's testimonial match I sat with George and David Sadler in the tea-room at Old Trafford. I didn't know he was not going to play in the match, otherwise I would have advised him to go out there for Bobby.

I will always remember George's brilliance, He knew what other players were capable of, and, when he was at his best, he was waiting for people to make mistakes. He knew who was liable to make them. One day at Old Trafford we took a throw-in which I had banned – a throw straight across the face of the pitch at the halfway line – and though I shouted, our fellow did the same thing again. George was reading it, and he flustered us into a mistake, sprinted through, picked up the ball and scored a goal. He made it happen. He started the trouble and then finished it off.

When George played his last game for Manchester United at Anfield he didn't play well and the crowd laughed at him. That was a terrible thing – because nobody could laugh at George Best.

Charlie George and I were friendly, too. Liverpool were at Highbury one day when Jimmy Hill took over as a linesman in an emergency. Charlie was Arsenal's substitute and I said to him, 'Hello, son, when are you going to stop this carry-on of tantrums and arguing with the referee? There's no good arguing with the referee. You can't win, son.'

He said, 'I've stopped it now.' Well, he hadn't really, because he had a lot of trouble after that. But he has now. He has settled in well with Derby.

If the ability of players like Best, Marsh, Bowles and George could be harnessed to collective team-play, I would have said, 'Play collectively and then I will give you a ten-minute spell on your own. OK, Stan, you can have five minutes' dribbling practice now!'

Throughout my career I preached to players that everything is all right in moderation. I kept harping on about it and I must have got through to them in the end. I always warned about the dangers of excess. Too many luxuries can make a man as soft as mush. Overeating and oversleeping can be just as bad as too much drink, too many cigarettes, too many late nights and too much sex.

Footballers are bound to attract women because they are young and fit and famous. Players are virile and alive, and sex in moderation does them good because it tones them down and makes them more relaxed.

The mental outlook plays such a big part in all this. Some fellows can go out and have their fun and their women and be happy and not give it a second thought. I knew a boy who had a lot of women and always played well. I knew others who would go with a woman only occasionally and would immediately suffer from attacks of conscience and play badly. The boy who says to himself, 'Oh, I shouldn't have done that last night,' is often the biggest problem.

On the other hand, the boys who overindulge are always a problem. An athlete should look like an athlete. His eyes should sparkle so much that you could light your cigarette from them or use them as car headlamps. Every Thursday morning at Melwood, Reuben Bennett, the Liverpool trainer, who was always full of wisecracks, used to look at the players' eyes and say: 'Where were you last night? You look as if you're going to die!'

We had no hard-and-fast rules. We relied on the common sense of the players themselves.

It would take another book to cover all the great players I have known. I have respect for them all, but some are never far from my mind. It is difficult to say who was the greatest player I ever saw, because so many were masters of their own particular positions and all my Liverpool players were supreme of course!

Tommy Finney was the best forward I ever saw in my life. He scored a couple of hundred goals for Preston and a lot of goals for England into the bargain, and I am certain that no player ever made more direct passes to a man to put the ball in the net. All calculated cut-backs from the byline. When people saw the Peles and the Cruyffs doing things like that they would say, 'Oh, brilliant.' Well, Tommy Finney was doing that when he was sixteen years old. If I were pressed into it, I would say Tommy was the best player ever born. But it is perhaps fairer to categorize, and say he was the best forward.

Stan Matthews was the great outside right, but Tommy scored more goals and was better in the air – there were ironical cheers if Stan headed a ball. Tommy was also a strong tackler – and George Best could tackle too. If anything, George could batter the ball harder than Tommy with either foot. Denis Law was like George for anticipating mistakes by the opposition. He seemed to know everything that was going to happen and would wait for it to happen and then make his move. He would wait for a man to head the ball down and would be on top of it and lash it into the net.

John Charles could play centre forward, inside forward, centre half, anywhere. He could be lurking about looking for chances, or coming forward from midfield, or backing up for crosses. You couldn't get near him. If John had possessed the spirit of Peter Doherty, then he would have been the greatest. Peter had wonderful skills and was toiling from the start to finish. He used to give me a hard game! Peter never gave in, because in his mind he was always winning. You could lace into him and harry him and flurry him, but you couldn't knock him off the ball. Law had a similar nature to Doherty's, and with that John Charles would probably have towered above everybody. I remember going over with Liverpool to play Juventus, and at their stadium in Turin we saw pictures of John on every table. There he was, up heading the ball – nearly heading the crossbar. They idolized him. He thrilled the life out of them.

When Jimmy Greaves ran any distance, thirty yards or more, you could bet your boots something was going to happen. I saw him at Tottenham once, when there was a flurry down the left side of the field. Jimmy knew the abilities of the players who were dealing with the ball and he made a sprint into the box. Sure enough, the ball came, and he poked it into the net. Jimmy belted the ball when he needed to belt it and pushed it when he needed to push it. He did everything right. When we played Tottenham I'd say: 'The nearest man to Greaves picks him up. We are not going to put one man on him and disrupt our plans. But whoever is the nearest man to Greaves must cotton on, because he is a dangerous bugger.' Jimmy and Roger Hunt were vying with each other for a place in the England team when we played at Tottenham once, and Roger scored a hat trick and was selected. Roger didn't only score goals, he also worked for other people. He ran his guts out for England.

Bobby Charlton was another player who worked like a slave. His distribution was wonderful. He could give long, raking passes and shoot with either foot. I couldn't tell whether he was right-footed or left-footed. He was so accurate, strong and dangerous.

My first season in the First Division with Preston was Alex James's last season. I played against him at Highbury. James was a genius. He would put Vaseline on his face and had a cocky countenance. He was a master player who just oozed confidence. Arsenal was the first team to be really organized and it was a nightmare playing against them. James was picking up the ball in midfield and poking it here and there. He would say to Ted Drake, 'Right, up, Ted.' Ted got the ball just outside the box and hit it. If our goalkeeper had got his hands to it it would have taken them off. Dear God, that shot was frightening. It nearly took the roof off the net. James, Drake, Cliff Bastin, Joe Hulme – what a team that was!

I also played against Hughie Gallacher, who was a menace. He was cunning and could get into positions where you couldn't catch him. He was more demonstrative than James, always talking, arguing and swearing to rile the opposition. He would say to big centre halves, 'How did you get on to the field? You won't get a kick of the ball today.' Everybody would be chasing after him, trying to kill him! He could beat half a dozen men with the ball by throwing dummies at them and caused panic and confusion by going to head the ball and then ducking out of the way. He could be on the field for half an hour without touching the ball and still have played a blinder by kidding people. James was small and thickset and Hughie was small and slender, but both were strong because they were strong-willed.

Raich Carter would have filled the net every season if he'd had Tommy Finney alongside him, rolling the ball back. Carter was arrogant. Once, when he played for Hull City, the ball was cut back for him and he lashed it with that left foot of his and turned round and walked away. He didn't even bother to watch, because he knew the ball was going in. Wilf Mannion was another player who had a fantastic brain, another genius who was alive to everything and knew all about the game.

Len Shackleton was like a cat playing with a mouse. He wanted to tantalize you without killing you off. He would put the ball through your legs and make a fool out of you. Once, before the start of a match, he stabbed the ball and, as it went away from him, he beckoned it with his finger and it came spinning right back to him. Bloody unbelievable. He would beat everybody, including the goalkeeper, and would stand at the goalpost until the goalkeeper ran back again and would then poke the ball in.

Dixie Dean and Tommy Lawton were on a par and it would be difficult to separate them. I saw more of Tommy than Dixie, though I played against Dixie for Preston against Everton. Tommy was a little taller and was maybe a little better on the floor and in the build-up. But the finishing was a different story.

Dixie was brilliant. People may reckon that some of his goals would have been ruled offside if they had been scored today, but his goals from the set pieces and the corner kicks wouldn't have been offside. Any great player then would have been a great player now, and vice versa, no matter what the system happened to be.

Billy Liddell, an idol of Liverpool, was tremendous and could play right, left or centre. I played for Scotland the day Billy and Willie Waddell made their debuts. Both were as strong as horses and could shoot. Matt Busby played in that match too. Matt had class, and was a wonderful kicker of a ball with his left foot – a great player.

When I was a boy my idol was Davie Meiklejohn, of Rangers, a centre half who made the game look easy. Davie was tall, but was not the big, rugged type. He was the really classy Scottish player people talk about, something on the style of Jim Baxter, but not as showy. Jimmy McGrory was at his peak with Celtic when Meiklejohn was playing, and Jimmy scored hundreds of goals, most of them with his head.

Though we were steeped in Rangers or Celtic, Motherwell played the most scientific football then; man-to-man stuff, precision passing. I was also lucky enough to see Alan Morton, one of Scotland's 'Blue Devils', a real wizard. Alec Massie was one of the best wing halves I saw. He played for Scotland in the position I took later. He was big, neat and clever. In his early days he was a bit of a fancy player, full of back heels and those kind of tricks, but later he realized he could do a little bit more than that, and would fight for the ball.

Joe Mercer played in the same position for Everton as I did for Preston, but Joe had more rope than I had. Preston played more methodical football, whereas Joe had more of a free hand to show his own individual play. Joe had a good temperament and liked a laugh, but that didn't mean he wasn't doing his job. Joe was always a pleasant-looking fellow, but others were sullen, like Jimmy Scoular, who was strong and could play too.

Stan Cullis was one of the great defenders and was a wonderful captain. No one could play cat-and-mouse with Cullis, who had a football brain which was equal to the one Alex James had. Duncan Edwards did not play long before tragedy overtook him at Munich, so we cannot know how great he would have been. I saw him when he was sixteen, and he had shoulders like a light-heavyweight. He had almost superhuman strength and was brilliant.

The game has been laced with wonderful goalkeepers, and a man who ranks with the best is Gordon Banks. Gordon played some marvellous games at Anfield and was always given a good reception by our supporters, as were many goalkeepers. Gordon's last League game was at Liverpool, the day before his road accident. I can't pay a greater tribute to Gordon than to add that I tried to sign him for Liverpool from Leicester before he went to Stoke City.

Of the foreign players, I will never forget a boy called Bican, an Austrian who was in the Czech team, Slavia, before the war. I played against Bican, and he was in the Puskas class, only bigger. Puskas had a left foot that could talk. The first time I saw two centre backs in play was when the Hungarians beat England 6–3 at Wembley. The Hungarians had a good side, but, no disrespect to them, I don't think they were up against a top-class England team. The system beat England – those two centre backs giving the full backs the chance to go wide on the wing and mark men, and Hidegkuti, the deep-lying centre forward. Hidegkuti could sway and twist and turn and beat men and – some people may laugh at this – was possibly a better centre forward than Di Stefano.

Having made that point, let me add that Di Stefano was one of the great individuals in a team that was a masterpiece. Di Stefano, Kopa and Gento – later joined by Puskas – played brilliant collective football for Real Madrid. Nobody talks about the defence, and yet the centre half, Santamaria, may have been even better than John Charles, and they had a player called Rial who was absolutely magnificent. They could have played in any era, in any season, in any conditions. That was the greatest team I have ever seen.

16 Auld Lang Syne

Life's a struggle from the cradle to the grave. I've been a slave to football. Every working man misses out on some things because of his job, and football demands a lifetime of dedication. You can never get away from it. It follows you home, it follows you everywhere, and eats into your family life.

I've had success, but a lot of genuine boys go through football without success. They don't have the luck to get the right opportunities at the right time, and I feel sorry for them. My opportunities came, but some came a little bit late. I have told of the things that happened in my career, and now I'll go into what might have been.

In 1951, when I was the manager of Carlisle United, I got a telephone call from Liverpool and was asked if I'd like to be interviewed for the manager's job. George Kay had just resigned. I stayed in Southport on the Sunday night and went to meet the Liverpool board the next day. I met Andy Beattie, who was then manager of Stockport, in Water Street.

I said, 'I know where you're going.'

'And I know where you're going,' said Andy.

When we had been interviewed and were picking up our expenses, we said in harmony, 'Well, I won't get it.'

On the train back to Carlisle I saw Scot Symon, who was travelling up to Scotland. It was obvious that he'd been for an interview as well. I didn't go and embarrass him by talking to him, because he would have been just as annoyed as Andy and myself at not getting the job, and probably for the same reason. The big snag had cropped up when the Liverpool board had said the manager could put down his team for matches and the directors would scrutinize it and alter it if they wanted to. So I just said, 'If I don't pick the team, what am I the manager of?' And that was that. Andy felt the same way.

I was just over thirty-six years old then. I had not long finished playing and I was young and fit and ambitious. Liverpool were in the First Division. They were struggling, but there were a lot of young players knocking about the game. I could have started the job eight years earlier than I did. God Almighty, what I would have done for Liverpool then! But a manager must be a manager. He is in charge of the players and the training staff. He organizes the training and the coaching, lays down the law – and picks the team. Without that he is nothing. The job went to Don Welsh and then Phil Taylor took over in 1957.

Shortly after that episode, when I was still at Carlisle, I was interviewed by West Bromwich Albion. I went to see them at a hotel in Derby. Major Wilson Keys was the chairman of West Brom. then. Vic Buckingham was also there for an interview. I remember he had a leather brief-case. Vic got the job.

I moved on to Grimsby, and after my first season, when we got sixty-six points but missed promotion, Middlesbrough interviewed me. I booked into a hotel at Ripon and went on up to Middlesbrough to see them in the evening. I was the only one interviewed and we didn't talk long. They said they wanted a young manager who could train with the team, and I thought, 'Well, that's it.' I didn't even bother to stay overnight in Ripon. I just picked up my stuff and went back home to Cleethorpes. I was excited about the job and went home and said to Ness, 'Well, there was only me there, so that's it.'

So I waited and waited, but nothing happened. I didn't hear from Middlesbrough and then they gave the job to somebody else. I've always felt that Arthur Drewry, a Grimsby director who was also president of the Football League, may have had a talk with the Middlesbrough chairman, Harry French, who was a member of the League Management Committee. I may be wrong, but I suspect Mr Drewry said, 'He's our manager, Harry.' My feeling about this was strengthened by the fact that Middlesbrough appointed Walter Rowley, from Bolton, who was getting on a bit compared to me and who was not a track-suit manager.

Missing that job was a terrible disappointment, because I was bubbling with ideas and Middlesbrough had a good ground and a lot of useful players. Before the war they'd had one of the best footballing teams in Britain. Ayresome Park represented potential, just as Liverpool did.

In 1953, when I was still at Grimsby, I went for an interview at Bradford Park Avenue. They were in the Third Division (North), but I felt they might have had potential. I didn't get the job, though I have learned since that I was on a short-list of two. And later, when I was at Huddersfield, I almost got a job at Leeds United before Jack Taylor took over. I think this fell through because Huddersfield and Leeds are a bit too close together for one to take a manager from the other.

It's strange how things work out, and I regret that I had to wait so long to get to a big club. I regret that I didn't get to Liverpool sooner, that I missed out at West Brom, and that things misfired at Middlesbrough. At the same time it is nice to know I can hold up my head if ever I go to Carlisle, Grimsby, Workington and Huddersfield. Ness and I made a lot of friends in all those places. The people were wonderful to us. We loved them all.

Ness and I are completely different and she knows absolutely nothing about football. She was brought up in a two-apartment house on the road to Celtic Park in the east end of Glasgow. Living conditions were difficult. There was only cold water and one toilet for four families. But her mother and father were one-hundred-per-cent honest and her mother was a strict disciplinarian. She made a good job of bringing up Ness and saw to it that she didn't take any wrong turnings. It is not easy to bring up a girl in a big city, and Ness has seen the rough and tumble of Glasgow and has heard the four-letter words since she was a foot high.

Her father, James Fisher, lived with us for the latter part of his life, about thirteen years. He was a motor-car engineer and during the wintertime when we lived in Huddersfield, and it was difficult for people to start their cars, half the people in the town seemed to send for Mr Fisher to help them.

Ness was well-educated and is intelligent and discreet. She never wants to offend anybody, but if she takes the needle she will go for people. She can lose her temper if provoked. She has never discouraged me from doing anything I have wanted to do. 'All right, go ahead and do it,' she will say. But she will give her opinion – and if I don't accept that opinion, it won't make any difference. Not a bit.

When I am blowing off steam she will say, 'I wouldn't say that,' and I will say, 'Oh, I'm only saying it to you.'

I might be murdering somebody with words, saying 'He's bloody rubbish!'

Ness will say, 'Don't say that to him.'

I will say, 'Oh, he can't hear us talking in our own lounge. He's a few miles away from here!'

As time went on and we were having a bit more success, Ness had a little more money to play with. She has taken to the Liverpool people because, coming from Glasgow, a similar city, she understands them. You couldn't meet a nicer person than Ness. She built up her friends and our daughters got married and were able to move into houses of their own, and we have grandchildren. Ness is never happier than when she is cooking for the whole family – and at least now I am able to see a little more of them all.

Liverpool was made for me and I was made for Liverpool, and I knew that the people who mattered most were the ones who came through the turnstiles. A manager has got to identify himself with the people. Football is their whole life, and for the last twelve seasons Liverpool have played two games most weeks, which is hard on the pocket.

The encouragement the supporters of Liverpool Football Club have given their team has been incredible. When there is a corner kick at the Kop end of the ground they frighten the ball! Occasionally I would have a walk round the ground before a match, and I went to the Kop one day before it had filled up. A little chap there said, 'Stand here, Bill, you'll get a good view of the game from here!' I couldn't take him up on that offer because I had to look after the team.

I have watched a match from the Kop since I retired as team manager, and that was just the start of going to see the supporters in all parts of the ground. I didn't go to the Kop for bravado or anything like that. I went as a mark of respect for people who had been good to me. They used to chant my name as much as they chanted the names of the players, which was unusual. I am a working man and I went among my own kind. Liverpool played Coventry that day, and a crescendo greeted the Liverpool team just as I went into the ground. It wasn't a great game and we only drew that day, so there wasn't a continuous din. But when we scored our goal the noise was deafening.

When I was the manager and the supporters were enjoying their jubilation I would be thinking about the next game or a player I was interested in signing. If one of the players wasn't playing well, I would be thinking, 'How long is he going to last?' Success brought happiness to the supporters and that was the great thing. But next day I would get out of my bed, thinking, 'Christ, there is another game next week,' or 'At the beginning of the new season we need this and we need that.' The manager never gets off the hook.

Supporters still come round to my house. In fact some have been many times. And since I retired from Anfield, the Everton supporters I have met couldn't have been nicer to me. When I have been at a function in the city they have said, 'I'm an Evertonian,' but, having made that point clear, they have stayed to talk with me. When I have been to matches at Everton, I have spoken to the boys on their way to the Gwladys Street end of Goodison, and they have put their arms around me, just like the Liverpool supporters. But whereas the Liverpool supporters did this as a sign of adulation, from the Everton boys it's a mark of respect. Because I had turned the tables on them – on Everton, the 'School of Science' – that's for sure!

Liverpool is full of show-business personalities, and I know them all. Ken Dodd lives not far from me and he's been down to Melwood and had some fun with the team, and Johnny Hackett and his wife are great friends of ours. Frankie Vaughan and Jimmy Tarbuck have both been in our dressing-room at Wembley, and Jimmy played a five-a-side match with us. He was on the losing side of course – he had no chance! You need humour in your life, and a football manager has to enjoy all the laughs he can get. I said that to Wilf McGuinness one day when he was manager of Manchester United. 'When you can get a laugh, Wilf, you take the chance, because you won't get many laughs.' And of course Wilf didn't get many laughs.

I have had some fun with the press boys too. I'd go to grounds like Tottenham's and maybe twenty of them would gather for a chat with me after a match. I'd say things like, 'Well, if you lot come every week Tottenham will be assured of a big crowd. Between you and that big board of directors, the stand will be full!' I hated to lose. If we had played well and lost, that wasn't so bad, but if we had not played well and had been beaten, it was a terrible disappointment. Some of the press boys would ask silly, amateurish questions, and would get some terrible answers. I think my weighing-up of people is not too bad. I would never embarrass anybody I thought was sensible, but if people tried to be clever or funny with me, I would tear them to pieces.

There was one particular guy in London who thought he was clever. When I was talking to the rest of the boys, he was leaning against a car, not bothering to listen, just sneering. I said to him, 'Who do you think you are? You think you know everything, do you? You might miss something. You should come over here and get educated.' In the end I made a remark that left him without a mother and a father. You get some newspaper-men who think they are exclusive because they are the leading football writers for their papers. They think they are above the rest. They think, 'I'm not going to listen to Bill Shankly or Matt Busby or Harry Catterick or Stan Cullis. I know better than them.'

That's a silly attitude because, no matter how big you think you are, you can learn from people in all walks of life. It is like playing football when someone else is in possession of the ball.

You run into position, and if you don't get a pass, you try running again and again until you do get one. You might run six times for nothing and get a pass the seventh time. If you don't do this your team plans can fall down. You can't just ignore what people say. You might go six times and not hear anything of interest, but the seventh time you might say to yourself, 'Christ, that's not bad.'

If a man is writing at a game, it is possible for him to miss something. I've seen men from other clubs vetting a team and all the time they are writing things down and drawing plans of movements. I feel like saying to them, 'Are you painting a picture? You've just missed something. Somebody has just done something bloody cute.' I would never take my eyes off the pitch for ninety minutes.

I have dealt with most of the newspaper-men and I have had rows with them – I said to one, 'I only see you once a year, and that's too bloody often!' – but in the main, if I had an argument with a pressman, that was it finished. I didn't harbour grudges. If anybody said anything about the Liverpool team, I saw red. Even if they were right, I would say they were wrong, if it was regarding a player or players. I would disagree with them in every aspect, while at the same time knowing full well that they were right. They might be right, but what they said would have been better unsaid.

The most amazing thing to me was the way they sniffed out stories. Something might be whispered somewhere and, within half an hour, somebody from the papers would be on the button. I said to one bloke, 'How the hell did you get any idea about this? And first and foremost I want to tell you it is wrong' – which meant it was right, of course! So a newspaper-man is also a kind of detective and most of them are characters.

Most men turn to the sports page first and leave the front-page news of wars and depressions until later. The reporter's job is to write the kind of stories that sell papers, and if you set a standard like Liverpool, Everton, Manchester United, Manchester City and the rest did, then people tend to expect you to win everything. But football can't do without the newspapers, because they create interest with articles about the personalities and news from the clubs, and this advertises the matches. Then there are the reports of matches, which people are always eager to read.

I can look back upon some wonderful times in football. I have an FA Cup winners' medal, a runners-up medal and a gold Charity Shield medal. I played for Scotland, and captained them once during the war, which was a tremendous honour. I was with Preston for sixteen years, and played ten full peacetime seasons for them. I didn't cause any trouble. I did everything I was asked to do, and possibly a bit more, and I played against some of the greatest men the game has seen.

As the manager of Liverpool, I got a cigarette box from the shareholders for winning the Second Division championship, and the League championship three times – we were also runners-up umpteen times – brought back the FA Cup twice (we were runners-up once) and won the UEFA Cup.

I was awarded the OBE, which was a reward for everyone's efforts, not only my own. Ladbrokes, the bookmakers, presented me with a silver statuette for services to sport. Arthur Dooley, the Liverpool sculptor, made a bust of me in bronze, which was given to me by the Variety Club of Great Britain. And Jap Van Praag, the president of Ajax, came all the way from Amsterdam to make the presentation. That was one of the most amazing things that happened to me – that that man, a millionaire, should take the time to do that. He said I was the only man in the world he would have done it for. 'When we beat Liverpool,' he said, 'I have never seen a man who was so defiant. He just said to me, "You haven't got a bloody team at all," ' and he really did believe Liverpool would beat us in the return game.'

Variety Club International made me a life member and gave me a silver plate. I have souvenirs from all the clubs we played in Europe – and I once managed to get the Manager of the Year trophy away from Don Revie. We won the championship three times and the FA Cup twice, and eventually I made it – I sneaked it for a year. Actually, the way that trophy was awarded rankled with me once or twice. In 1970 Harry Catterick won the League championship for Everton and his team had played good football. The Manager of the Year presentation, organized by Bell's, the whisky firm, was made in Glasgow, on the eve of an international match. I went up for the match but I didn't go to the presentation. I met one of the pressmen at the hotel and asked him who had won it. He told me it was Don Revie, and that surprised me. I'm not saying anything against Don Revie, and Leeds United were great. But that year, though they had been involved in everything, Leeds had won nothing. It must have been a terrible blow for a fellow like Harry, who had just won his second championship.

In 1973, when Liverpool won the League and the UEFA Cup, I received the *Sun* Award of Manager of the Year, and I have also received a silver star from the Vaux brewery company and was the subject of *This Is Your Life* on television. But my greatest treasures are memories, and what means most to me is the fact that Anfield is my memorial. When I came to Liverpool, the ground was a shambles. Now it is neat, with three new stands and good facilities. It is a good set-up with a good team. When I go to Anfield now, that is the reward. I can sit there and say to myself, 'I have had something to do with this.'

Sometimes, when I am at home instead of being out training or playing five-a-side games, or working on my chat show at Radio City, or speaking at functions, or helping somebody in football, or doing one of the million and one things that occupy my time now, I play some of my records. The one that gives me the most pleasure is a recording by a folk group of 'Amazing Grace', only the words are all about Bill Shankly. That is a wonderful tribute to me. When I am out amongst the people and they are so enthusiastic and friendly, wearing red scarves and rushing up for autographs and to speak to me, it is a bonus.

I would like to be remembered, first and foremost, as a man who looked after his family. I would also like people to say that I created something through hard work and never cheated anybody. When I was a player at Preston, they were anxious to win matches, and so were the clubs I managed. The clubs were anxious and the supporters were anxious. And I was just as anxious. I would like people to say that I played the game with them, that I was fair and that I helped more people than I hindered. If I was harsh with people, then those people deserved it. But I have always tried to help.

There were two little boys hiding in the toilet of a train so that the ticket-collector wouldn't find them, and I paid their fare. Another time I was on a train coming back from London, having a cup of tea with a couple of Everton supporters who didn't have tickets, and I told the inspector, 'They are all right. They are with me.' He let them go, and when we arrived at Lime Street, they nearly broke the hundred yards' record and then jumped over a bloody wall! And there was a fellow called Big Benny, who has gone now unfortunately. Benny used to support both Everton and Liverpool. He used to come to see me for a chat and I would get him tickets for matches. I would give people anything within reason.

Above all I would like to be remembered as a man who was selfless, who strived and worried so that others could share the glory, and who built up a family of people who could hold their heads high and say, 'We're Liverpool.'

Ever since I can remember there has been nothing but pessimism in the world. There has never been enough optimism. People have always said, 'We'll starve – we're doomed.' But we're still here.

In football you will always find that when the FA Cup comes along, a little team, from the Fourth Division, will beat a big team. If the little team played all their games the way they played the Cup-tie they would be out of the Fourth Division. Complacency is the killer. If every player in every match – irrespective of what was at stake – played as if he was in a cup-tie, then I think the crowds would be bigger. Too often you will see a team in a cup-tie hell-bent on winning and giving full value – then next time, when you see them in a League match, they are trash. I have seen great club players in international matches and something has been missing in their game, perhaps because they are playing for themselves instead of giving everything for the team. If football was booming in this country, the country might be better off.

You can only help others by being strong – though a lot of people in positions of strength don't help anybody, bar themselves. If everybody put all their ability and enthusiasm into their jobs, life would be better. It might be a lousy job, like scrubbing tables or scrubbing floors, but do it, for God's sake! Thieves can come in the night and pilfer all your possessions, but no one can take what you have inside you.

My sister Jean, the mother of Roger Hynd, the Birmingham City player, died a couple of years ago, but Liz, Netta, Belle and Barbara still live in Scotland, along with my brothers Bob and Jimmy. Bob is still busy as a director and general manager of Stirling Albion, and has worked hard all his life. The highlight of his career was the great team he had at Dundee, and he is very friendly with Jock Stein. They are very similar men.

Jimmy is a great optimist. In fact of all the men I have met in my life – and I have met a lot of famous people – I would say Jimmy is the best example of what a man should be. He kept our family going by sending money when he played football in England, and also spread kindness amongst others. He has never looked on the black side and has always laughed at set-backs.

My mother was the greatest optimist of all, of course, and I place her above everyone. Some people are tired because they want to be tired, but my mother had the most marvellous philosophy. She used to say, 'If you've got your health and strength, every day you get out of bed is a holiday.'